The
Defiant
Child

A PARENT'S GUIDE TO

OPPOSITIONAL DEFIANT DISORDER

Dr. Douglas Riley

TAYLOR TRADE PUBLISHING

Lanham • New York • Oxford

Published by Taylor Trade Publishing
4720 Boston Way
Lanham, Maryland 20706

Distributed by National Book Network

The author gratefully thanks the American Psychiatric Association
for permission to quote the passage from its *Diagnostic and Statistical Manual of
Mental Disorders, Fourth Edition* that appears on page 2.

Book design by Mark McGarry
Set in Nofret & Officiana Sans

Library of Congress Cataloging-in-Publication Data
Riley, Douglas.
The defiant child : a parents guide to
oppositional defiant disorder / Douglas Riley.
p. cm. Includes index
ISBN 0-87833-963-9
1. Oppositional defiant disorder in children – Popular works.
2. Oppositional defiant disorder in adolescence – Popular works. I. Title.
RJ50+.066R54 1997
618.92'89 – dc21 97-24358
CIP

Printed in the United States of America

To the memory of my parents,
Nellie Cothran Riley and Basil Deward Riley.
Thank you for everything you taught me.

| CONTENTS |

| ACKNOWLEDGMENTS |

MANY PEOPLE deserve recognition for the contributions they have made to my understanding of children and adolescents. In a real sense they are partners in this book, and I am happy to have the chance to acknowledge them publicly.

The Department of Counselor Education and Counseling Psychology at Western Michigan University, where I received my graduate education, generously supported me over a number of years with grants and assistantships. I hope that this book reflects positively on the department.

My mentor at Western Michigan, Dr. Robert Betz, taught me to think about thinking. Although the mistakes in this book are most assuredly my own, his influence can be seen throughout the sections that emphasize that behavior cannot be changed without looking at the thought behind the behavior.

Several colleagues deserve mention. Dr. Charles Lowe, Dr. Tom Lanning, and John Vesey, MSW, have for years shared their insight into how children and adolescents, particularly those of the opposi-tional variety, behave and think. I am particularly indebted to Dr. Carolyn Wilson-Garrison and David Linn, ACSW, of Kalamazoo Clinical Associates, my former business partners, for their insight into analytic psychology and family systems theory. I also must take the opportunity to thank Dr. John Hogg and the physicians, nurses, and staff at The Children's Clinic in Newport News, Virginia, for their support of my current endeavors.

I wish to thank Taylor Publishing. My editor, Jason Rath, approached the editing process with keen insight into psychological material. His questions and suggestions for clarification improved the manuscript in many ways.

I also wish to thank the parents of the children and teenagers I work with. Being allowed into the world of a child is a privileged position, and I have been honored over the years by parents who have extended their trust to me.

There is no possible way this book could have been completed without the forbearance and support of my wife, Debra Lintz-Riley, and my sons, Collin and Sam, the two best boys in the whole world.

| INTRODUCTION |

FOR JUST a few minutes, allow me to skip the technical and scientific descriptions of oppositional defiant disorder (we'll get to those in chapter one). Chances are you already know what oppositional defiant disorder is like if you (1) were ever a child or teenager yourself, or (2) if you have a child or teenager living in your house. Oppositional defiant disorder is an exaggerated attempt on the part of a child or teenager to prove to you that you don't have any power over them. Most of us have acted this way before to one extent or another.

When mental health professionals talk about the term oppositional defiant disorder, the word of most concern to parents is typically *disorder*. It is a word fraught with negative connotations implying that the child has some sort of disease that parents are somehow responsible for. If I had the power to change the diagnostic labels we use in the field of psychology, I would change the term to oppositional defiant spectrum.

Why spectrum? The reason, simply enough, is that every child and teenager displays oppositional, defiant behavior at some point. Some display it to a degree that is more reasonably termed an occasional irritation than a disorder. Others, however, display it with such frequency and intensity that it keeps them in constant trouble with parents, teachers, and legal authorities.

There is good news implied in this notion of a spectrum. The best news is that oppositional behavior should rarely be viewed as a mental illness in the same way that schizophrenia, manic depression, or multiple personality disorder can be seen as mental illnesses. To put it another way, most of the people you meet who are schizophrenic are mentally ill and, barring medical miracles, are likely to stay that way. Few of the children and teenagers you meet who display oppositional behavior are mentally ill in the traditional sense of the word. In fact, under the right conditions and circumstances, they quickly change their behavior.

This book is my attempt to explain how parents can set up the right conditions and circumstances to help oppositional children and teenagers change their behavior. Be prepared for them to resist change and to ignore your attempts to use reason and logic to convince them. They believe that if they ignore you, they can just keep doing what they do. This book is about how you can talk to your oppositional child and what you can do once talk has failed.

I'm optimistic about the outcome for oppositional children and teenagers once parents begin to use the methods I've described in this book. Over the years I've seen many of them change from surly and combative to cooperative and productive. Part of my reason for optimism is that oppositional children and teenagers are often quite bright, creative, and vigorous. These are characteristics that bode well for long-term success, and with the right kind of help, that's what your oppositional child can achieve.

| CHAPTER ONE |

Understanding the Defiant Child

WHENEVER I think about the defiant child, I think about Tom. When I first met Tom, he was sixteen years old and had skipped most of the first semester of his sophomore year in high school. His father, a research scientist, informed me on the phone that Tom had driven most of his teachers close to assault with his mouth and his attitude. Although he was bright, he was headed down a path that would leave him lucky to graduate. He had just been arrested at a friend's home, along with several other boys his age.

Soon after the friend's parents left for dinner and a movie, a party had broken out. Tom and his friends got drunk and cranked up the stereo. A neighbor phoned in a complaint. When the police came, Tom grabbed one of them by the arm. He was charged with assault and resisting arrest and, from my viewpoint, was lucky to have run into a police officer not quick to respond with force.

When I walked out into my waiting room to meet Tom, I saw a tall, rangy, pimply faced young man sitting in a chair, reading one of the magazines on my coffee table. I introduced myself to him and

| 1

asked him to come back to my office. He responded by refusing to look at me or speak and continued to read.

Having learned long ago not to get into confrontations such as these, I told Tom that he could come back to my office when he pleased. I also added that his father might find it interesting to learn that he was paying good money to have Tom just sit in my waiting room and look at magazines.

Tom found his way back to my office after about ten minutes. His first words to me were that he didn't intend to listen to anything I had to say. He explained that psychology was not a real science, like physics or chemistry, so there was nothing I could tell him that was of any value. Then he sat down and began to read my magazine again.

The diagnostic term that psychologists use for young people like Tom is oppositional defiant disorder. They come in all ages, sizes, races, all social backgrounds, and from both sexes. The American Psychiatric Association's *Diagnostic and Statistical Manual of Mental Disorders, Fourth Edition*, uses the following criteria to describe their behavior:

A pattern of negativistic, hostile, and defiant behavior lasting at least six months, during which four (or more) of the following are present:

- often loses temper
- often argues with adults
- often actively defies or refuses to comply with adults' requests or rules
- often deliberately annoys people
- often blames others for his or her mistakes or misbehaviors
- is often touchy or easily annoyed by others
- is often angry and resentful
- is often spiteful or vindictive

It is important to note that normal childhood attempts to defeat authority do not constitute full-blown oppositional states. The behaviors noted above should occur at a rate and intensity far beyond that seen in the subject's peers and should be of such magnitude that they create noticeable difficulties in social, academic, and occupational functioning.

Children pass through several stages as they mature, stages in which they challenge your authority, in which they question your most cherished beliefs. It is appropriate for a child to push the limits set down by the parents; if they don't push against them, they will not know where they are. It should come as no surprise that sometimes the preacher's kid goes through a period of being profane, the police officer's through a period of vandalism, the teacher's through a period of academic failure. Such episodes should not be seen as parenting failures. They are just the results of young people testing the limits of their worlds.

It becomes important to understand what represents a "normal" amount of oppositional behavior and where the boundary of "normal" ends. In general, oppositional children have a drive to defeat adults that assumes absurd proportions. They are as relentless as gravity in their pursuit of proving adults to be wrong, stupid, or both.

To fully understand the behavior of oppositional children, we first have to understand how they think and how they see the world. Below I outline several "rules" for comprehending the behavior and thought patterns of oppositional children. These should help you realize that, as with any system of irrational or disturbed thinking, the person acting is not aware that he is coming to irrational conclusions or behaving in an irrational manner. Also, you will see one additional theme threaded through each of these guidelines: The dominant thoughts of the oppositional child revolve around defeating anyone's attempt to exercise authority over him. If you were to ask an oppositional child if this is how he thinks, he would probably deny it. If you were to ask his parents if this is how their child behaves, most would say, "That's my kid." This insight will be key to understanding and dealing with the oppositional child.

RULE 1: OPPOSITIONAL CHILDREN LIVE IN A FANTASY LAND IN WHICH THEY ARE ABLE TO DEFEAT ALL AUTHORITY FIGURES.

For some children and teenagers, a fantasy land in which they always defeat adults is a much more interesting place than reality. One description I've heard from parents goes like this: "It doesn't matter what I do. I can spank her, ground her, yell at her, or take things away. I could take away everything she owns, but nothing seems to get to her. I can talk till I'm blue in the face."

When a child or teenager is living in oppositional fantasy land, he may as well be living in another dimension. It seems like your messages, requests, and demands take light years to register. I worked with one young woman, for example, whose personal style revolved around black fingernail polish, jet black dyed hair, multiple crucifixes, miniskirts, and workboots. I could say to her, "It looks like a nice day outside," and she would say, "Only if you're stupid enough to think the sun is good for you." I would say, "I hope you have a good weekend," and she returned with, "Fun is for people who can't think." I found little to say that she did not disagree with in order to show me that I could not influence her in any way. I suspect that in her mind each of her put-downs constituted a mark in the victory column.

I couldn't take it personally because she treated everyone this way. In the words of a comedian I once heard on television, she was an equal opportunity offender. She would engage in such adversarial conversation with anyone–whether it was me, her parents, or her teachers. This is not to say that I condoned her behavior. As this book unfolds you will find that I am a firm believer in setting limits and imposing consequences for rude behavior. But I also believe that oppositional behavior must first be understood before it can attempt be controlled.

RULE 2: OPPOSITIONAL CHILDREN ARE OPTIMISTIC.

Russel believed that, since he didn't want to see me, the best thing to do was to beat me up. He was nine and weighed in at almost seventy-five pounds. I'm somewhat older than nine and weigh in at just a tad more. Russel tried to twist my wrist and tried to grab my tie and tie it in a knot. "OK," he said, " just you and me, outside!" Russel, by anyone's standards, was being optimistic.

Rule two grows out of rule one, in that oppositional children and teenagers see every interaction with adults as a win–lose proposition, are vigorously intent on winning, and would not be willing to continually take on adults, particularly those willing to punish them, unless they had at least some hope for success. It is the optimistic fantasy of victory that sets them free to engage so many adults in battle. This is warped optimism, but optimism nonetheless.

Oppositional optimism is often directed toward a particular goal. Michelle had it as her goal to get kicked out of school in her freshman year so that she would be sent to alternative education, a program that she mistakenly believed would make no demands on her. In order to get what she wanted, she skipped classes, beat up other girls in the hallways, and had nothing but a surly attitude toward anyone who attempted to engage her.

Michelle loved to give me a list of the people she had done battle with each week. Her blue eyes would crackle, and she would put her chubby fingers over her mouth when she giggled, displaying her notably large collection of cheap rings. Her straw-colored hair frizzed outward, giving her the appearance of being electrified. The only time I saw her animated like this was when she was recounting the week's victories, and she made me realize that happy must be the warrior who, in her own mind, never fails.

It is not just the unfriendly and aggressive child or teenager who is oppositional. I recently had a conversation with a merry little nine-year-old who initially saw me after deciding that he didn't have to do chores any longer because if he couldn't give his parents chores, neither could they give them to him. We were at a stage of therapy in which I help children begin to examine their decision-making process. We were talking about how he had to learn to stay calm when his parents told him "No." His tendency had been to either flip out or pitch a crying jag, and we were talking about how big guys like himself had to learn to just accept his parent's answer. I used the example, "What if you wanted some jelly beans and your parents told you 'No,' what would you do?"

"I'd wait until they were upstairs or in the shower, and then I'd take them."

"That might get you into big trouble."

"I'd get away with it because they wouldn't see me."

"What if your brother or sister saw you."

"Then I'd only take one while they were watching, because they wouldn't care if I only took one. Then when they weren't watching I'd take the bag and hide it under my bed."

"What if your mom or dad found it under your bed?"

"I'd tell them someone else put it there."

And so on.

For every possible consequence I could come up with, he had a ready answer. The defining character of all of his answers was that he would defeat the adults by use of strategy, guile, cunning, or lying. Every oppositional child and teenager I know has this oppositional optimism, this belief that they will defeat authority's attempt to control them or limit their behavior.

What follows is my memory of a conversation about running away from home that I've had with what seems like hundreds of teenagers over the years. The faces change, but the conversation remains the same. It's as if there is some universal faulty-logic gene that gets inserted into oppositional kids' DNA at conception.

"I'm going to run away from home."

"You'll create more problems for yourself than you'll solve. After you run away, your parents will call the police, and they'll put out a warrant for you."

"They can't catch me."

"I've known fifty people your age who told me they wouldn't get caught, and they all ended up in the juvenile home. They got caught."

"But I won't."

"Why not?"

"I'm too fast [or substitute 'smart'] to get caught."

"That's what the other ones thought."

"I'm faster [or 'smarter'] than they are."

Rule 3: Oppositional Children Fail to Learn from Experience.

Michelle failed to learn from experience because she viewed the world through the distortions of oppositional victory. She displayed little if any insight into why her parents were constantly angry with her, why her teachers cut her little slack, and why she was always the first to be blamed when trouble arose. She continued to run with a group of peers who stole several hundred dollars worth of her mother's jewelry one night when her parents were trusting enough to leave her at home while they were out. Her parents, in an act of sheer frustration, invited their own friends over one evening when she was gone and asked them to please go into her room and take anything they would like to have. Even in the face of such parental interventions, Michelle continued to break every rule imaginable. Like most oppositional children, when pressed to explain why she was always in so much trouble with the adults around her, she relied on the conspiracy theory. "Everyone has it in for me," she would say. "I don't know why."

Our girl in black has also failed to learn from experience. She is bright, a talented artist, and quick witted. But she describes everything around her as dumb and every adult around her as stupid. She adamantly insists that all the things everyone else seems to enjoy are boring to her, and she has gone everywhere and seen everything there is to see. She finds that no friends call, and she is rarely asked out for a date. She is depressed, but her medications have thus far offered her little relief. She is unwilling to believe that the way she thinks has a negative effect on her or on others.

RULE 4: YOU MUST BE FAIR TO ME, REGARDLESS OF HOW I TREAT YOU.

John was fifteen, looked eighteen, and behaved like a thirty-year-old criminal. He had a surly disposition and was devoid of the urge to return any nicety you might extend to him. He would just stare at you and smirk if you asked him how he was doing.

John was not reciprocal, meaning that he felt no more need to interact with human beings than the proverbial junkyard dog. John saw people as object or as function, meaning that he was concerned only with what you could provide him or do for him. He took it as a given that he had to do nothing for you. When I met John he was failing school miserably, had alienated all of his teachers, had learned to manipulate his mother by threatening to hit her, and was skipping school on a regular basis.

He had shoved his English teacher in the classroom one day and was sent to the office. Because he had been in the office most of the day, he failed to hand in an English assignment and his teacher refused to accept it the next day. John was outraged that his teacher, the same woman he had shoved, refused to accept his assignment and could simply not understand when I indicated to him that not accepting the paper was probably the teacher's way of getting revenge. He sputtered for a second, the only time I saw him lose his composure. "Teachers," he said, "are supposed to be fair."

You can't take John's behavior personally, because if you did you would want to clobber him. The desire on the part of adults to whack kids like John (at fifteen he could hardly be considered any- thing other than a child, regardless of his size and thugish attitude) exposes the underbelly of many adults' responses to oppositional children.

Although thoughtful adults are rightfully troubled by the urge to clobber a kid, they can at least see the strength of the urge as a barometer of just how oppositional the child is. When oppositional behavior and lack of concern about reciprocity and fairness collide with an adult's attempt to be nice or fair, the typical adult response is to feel taken advantage of.

Take the case of Ryan, a classically handsome high school senior who was athletically gifted, remarkably popular, and at least smart enough to get by in high school. He had come to the conclusion that, at eighteen, he no longer needed to pay attention to what his parents had to say. He maintained this attitude despite the fact that they pur- chased a car for him, purchased most of his clothing, gave him most of his spending money, and took care of him in every other way.

On his eighteenth birthday, Ryan's parents threw a surprise party for him. During the course of the party, he and his friends decided to have fun by stomping on the popcorn and potato chips. Afterward, they decided to leave early to go elsewhere and have some real fun.

His response to his parents' request that he help clean up the chips was that he hadn't asked for the party to begin with so he wasn't responsible for its aftermath. To say that his parents wanted to clobber him is an understatement, but to say that Ryan was a bit lacking in empathy and fairness toward them would also be an understatement.

It is well known in the folklore of child psychology that many of the victims of childhood physical abuse are oppositional children who are unfortunate enough to live with adults who cannot contain their own fantasies of revenge. This in itself may be the root cause of the next rule.

Rule 5: Oppositional Children Seek Revenge When Angered.

I saw a boy a number of years ago who could be described as a red-headed dynamo. When sitting (something he rarely did), he looked cute. There was nothing cute about his attitude, however. At age five he was ruling his parents through his demanding, negativistic manner, and any attempt on their part to punish or control him resulted in intense tantrums, name calling, hitting, spitting, biting, and kicking. His parents, both haggard twenty-five-year-olds, told me that they had no control over him.

I got a chance to witness their lack of control first hand during our initial meeting. When it came time to go back to my office, he hid under one of the chairs in my waiting room and refused to come out. Over the next few minutes, no amount of coaxing, reasoning, or bribing could move him. He simply sat there. The parents looked at me, defeated, and indicated that there was nothing they could do. I told them that, were he my child, I would pick him up and carry him back to the office. Then I would do whatever was necessary to keep him there. The child seemed momentarily stunned when his father pulled him out from under the chair, then unleashed a torrent of yelling and threats on the way down the hallway in his father's arms. As might be expected, once they put him down in my office, he headed straight for the door. Both parents looked at me, as if seeking my permission, and then hauled him back in the room. His mood at that point seemed something akin to a wet tomcat. They asked me what they should do, because it was apparent that once they let him go he would simply head back to the door.

My response was that if they knew he would go back to the door, it would be foolish to let him go until he made a firm promise to stay away from the door. Both parents wanted to know if doing something like that wasn't abusive, and I assured them that it was not. I explained that all they were doing was re-establishing themselves as the ones in charge. We talked about the idea that a home commanded by a five-year-old is the emotional equivalent of allowing that same child to drive the family home at the end of the session. The outcome of each situation is equally predictable.

During the next twenty minutes, each parent took turns holding the child, with him yelling and making threats all the while. At the end of twenty minutes he was slick with sweat, and he finally promised that he would sit and talk about his behavior at home.

We were amazed. He showed a clear awareness of how his behavior was different from that of other kids his age, and he was aware that it needed to change. We ended the session on what I believed to be friendly terms, and I walked with the redhead and his parents back out into the waiting area. He asked to use the bathroom, which was adjacent to the waiting area, and I spoke with his parents until he returned.

This was one of those situations where intuition took over, and I asked his parents to wait for a second while I checked my bathroom. It was wrecked. He had poured water on the floor, then had thrown toilet paper into the puddle of water. The tissue box atop the toilet was emptied into the sink. He had tipped over the trash can. He had, quite clearly, taken revenge on me for my role in having his parents control him during the visit.

RULE 6: OPPOSITIONAL CHILDREN NEED TO FEEL TOUGH.

This rule is reserved primarily for extremely oppositional teenagers—the ones who truly seem to warrant the label sociopath. Jim provides a good example. He came from a family that valued being tough above all other qualities. His description of a normal week included several fights, riding his motorcycle more than one hundred thirty miles per hour, and seeing how many people he could knock out at football practice.

In the summer I first met him, there had been an outbreak of young males from different high schools beating each other up. This may sound like typical school rivalry, but it had taken a nasty turn. The pattern was for several boys to jump a boy they found alone, the several often armed with baseball bats. Jim had himself been attacked one night while sitting in his car at a fast food restaurant. Someone had come up to his open window, said "Hey!" and hit him square in the face when he turned his head. His response was to grab his car jack handle and go after the assailant and his friends. They tried to get in their own car and leave, but not before Jim had put some good dents in it.

In Jim's mind, this level of response was absolutely necessary. For him to respond in any other way would have been an act of cowardice. Although the merits of this philosophy may be debated, it becomes a problem when such an attitude colors a child or teenager's interactions with *everyone*. Jim always had to respond with force, whether it was hitting his younger brother for not giving him the TV remote control or hitting his little sister for talking back to him. The few times he exposed his deeper thoughts and emotions, they revolved around the idea that it was necessary to prove that no one could make him do anything. He could not articulate why this was important and seemed mystified that not everyone followed his line of logic. To him, everything seemed so clear.

RULE 7: OPPOSITIONAL CHILDREN BELIEVE THAT IF THEY IGNORE YOU LONG ENOUGH, YOU'LL RUN OUT OF MOVES.

Every parent of an oppositional child is aware of this rule, whether or not they have heard it stated this clearly. Oppositional children believe that if they ignore their parents' attempts to use reason and logic, then the parents have nothing left to do. No moves left, so to speak. For example, if you tell your oppositional child not to turn on the TV, he likely believes at some level that, if he just ignores you, he has a fair chance of getting away with watching it anyway. The cycle goes something like this: You talk, he ignores. You talk more, he ignores. And so on. Pretty soon you, too, may come to believe that you have no moves left.

Sandy, an oppositional fifteen-year-old I first saw because she had been caught shoplifting, had a habit of sneaking downstairs late at night, taking the keys to the family car, and joy riding with her friends. Sandy's parents had caught her stealing the car before and gave her a stern warning not to do it ever again. They used reason and logic, such as "You're an uninsured driver and if you killed someone we'd be sued for everything we owned." Sandy ignored such reasoning, as oppositional children do. Apparently, she felt her parents would eventually run out of moves.

At some point, Sandy's parents bought a new car. As you might guess, they gave her stern warnings about stealing the new car, and they probably used lots of reason and logic. Sandy swore she would not touch the new car, a promise that lasted for about four nights. She took the car, picked up her friends, and somehow managed to blow out a rear tire. Because the car was a front wheel drive model, they were able to drive it home and park it in the driveway. It listed badly to the right, since by now the right rear tire had come all of the way off and the wheel cover was gone. All that remained was the rim.

The next morning, Sandy's mother accused her of having something to do with the damaged car, but Sandy was an expert at covering her own tracks when the pressure was on. She explained to her mother that the blowout must have occurred the day before when her mother was driving home from work. Since the new car had front wheel drive and excellent suspension, she probably hadn't even noticed the loss. Her mother, fair-minded soul that she was, accepted this explanation.

They had an appointment with me a few days after all of this. In the course of our conversation the story about the blown tire came up. My response was to laugh. If I recall, I didn't just laugh, I laughed until I had tears in my eyes. Sandy was gesturing to me frantically to shut up. Her mother's eyes became wide, round, and focused.

That evening, Sandy's parents confronted her, at which time she tearfully and dramatically claimed to have finally learned her lesson. She assured her parents that she would never take the car again, but her parents had finally learned that their trust was misplaced. They made a deal with each other to keep watch during the next few nights, and soon enough they heard her sneak out of the house and take the car. She was gone for about two hours, drove back in the driveway, re-entered the house, and went back into her bedroom. After she was asleep, her parents went into her bedroom and cut off her bangs. (A bit of history: This all occurred at a time when girls in her area wore rather extravagant bangs, modeled after the actress Farrah Fawcett from the television show *Charlie's Angels*. For Sandy and her friends, their bangs were their pride and joy.)

Her parents told me that they heard a scream after Sandy got up, a lot of banging around and doors slamming, and then she came down to breakfast wearing a ski cap. She didn't say anything to them about her bangs. They didn't say anything to her about their car. They all ate in silence, and then the mother took Sandy and the other children to school.

Sandy's parents went beyond reason and logic. Although I could not necessarily condone what they did, I did not fail to notice that Sandy did not steal the car again. She no longer believed that if she ignored her parents long enough, they would have no moves left.

This particular story, by the way, had a happy ending. About a year after we had completed counseling, Sandy dropped by my office to say hello. She was on the B honor roll at school and was playing on the softball team. Her parents had begun to trust her, and she was making plans to study nursing after graduation.

RULE 8: OPPOSITIONAL CHILDREN BELIEVE THEMSELVES TO BE EQUAL TO THEIR PARENTS.

I frequently hear oppositional teenagers tell their parents, "If you ground me, I'll just leave." There have to be several hundred variations of this statement. "I'll leave if I want to, and you can't stop me." Or, "I'm sixteen and have the right to make my own decisions."

A less in-your-face version of this starts with "I don't understand why . . . " For example, "I'm sixteen; I don't understand why I have to tell you where I'm going." Or, "I know he's twenty-two, but I don't understand why I can't date him."

In either of these cases, the in-your-face version or the more socialized, logic-oriented version, the message is that the oppositional child sees herself as your equal.

This feeling of equality is what separates a normal teenager's instincts to exercise power from the oppositional teenager's exercise of power. Although the nonoppositional child will debate with you about your decisions—even argue vigorously—the oppositional child will do as she pleases without explanation because she believes she is your equal.

All of the children and teenagers we've discussed thus far had the (mistaken) belief that they were equal to the adults in their lives and had the same rights as the adults. Ryan, our potato chip smasher, was often civilized and friendly in his oppositionality, but if he didn't want to go to school, he simply didn't. "It's my right," he'd say. If his plans interfered with the family's, too bad. I asked him on several occasions what would happen if he failed to do something he knew was important to his parents, perhaps even demanded by them. "Nothing," he'd say. Or, "They'll get over it."

John, the boy who pushed his teacher, didn't believe that he had to check with his mother on anything he wanted to do. Because she was afraid of him, he essentially had no curfew and no responsibilities. He believed that he had the right not to have to explain himself in any way and the right not to have to ask his mother's permission for anything.

The little boy who wrecked my office bathroom was another good example of a young man who did not think he needed to comply with parental requests. Even though he was very young, he clearly displayed a belief shared by Ryan and John that he had as much right to disobey his parents as they had to tell him what to do.

Oppositional children and teenagers consistently fail to respect how experience helps determine the roles different people are able to play. One fourteen-year-old I presently see tells me he is a better football player than Deion Sanders of the Dallas Cowboys. He sees himself as Sanders's equal without pausing to think that, although he is a talented athlete, he doesn't have the experience necessary to occupy Sanders's role. Neither does he consider what he must do to gain that experience. His oppositionality allows him to think of himself as Sanders's equal even though he hasn't played organized sports for several years because it takes away from the time he spends with his friends at the mall. This boy is also a good example of the behaviors displayed by oppositional children who hold the strong belief that they are your equals. They tend to slouch way down in the chair when speaking to adult authority figures, the same way they might slouch when talking with their friends. They tend to spit when you talk to them outside or use the same profane language they use with their friends. The bolder ones pull out a cigarette and ask for a light. I remember one young man asking if I could arrange to buy him some marijuana, given that I probably had a few drug dealers for patients.

An aspect of this assumed equality seems to be that age differences do not matter. Fourteen-year-olds may believe that their opinions should carry equal authority as those of parents, teachers, and others. Although most teenagers go through this stage, the oppositional child, as with everything else, takes it to the extreme.

Jennie, who is fifteen, physically developed, and enamored of drug dealers and other young men who populate the fast lane, tells me that there's no reason she shouldn't date twenty-year-old men. She tells me that if she were thirty and her boyfriend thirty-five, I wouldn't have anything to say. Five years difference in age, she says, is no big deal.

I tell her she's right in some ways and explain to her that the difference between thirty and thirty-five can be expressed visually as being about two inches. The difference between fifteen and twenty, however, is more like two yards.

I should add that it is a common characteristic for the physically mature oppositional fifteen-year-old female to date twenty to twenty-five-year-old males. For them, it is an extreme sign of status to go out with such an older male, regardless of the sexual abuse usually present in such relationships.

When the oppositional girls I work with tell me they are dating someone who is, say, twenty-one, I ask them, "What's wrong with him?" The conversation usually then goes like this:

"What do you mean, what's wrong with him?"

"There's something wrong with any man that age who is attracted to girls your age."

"What makes you say that?"

"If there wasn't something wrong with him he'd be dating women his own age."

You can see where this conversation might lead. Jennie will insist that she already knows enough about life and that five more years of growth and development will not change her in the least. I challenge her to go talk to a twenty-year-old female and ask her if she was as mature at fifteen as she is at twenty.

Also, don't make the mistake of thinking that this sense of equality comes only with teenagers. Although it becomes highly pronounced around age fifteen, it can easily be seen in much younger children. "Mother!" I heard one nine-year-old recently shout at a soccer game, "You're treating me like a child."

"That's what I thought you were," her mother replied.

RULE 9: OPPOSITIONAL CHILDREN FROM MIDDLE-CLASS HOMES EMULATE THE BEHAVIOR OF THEIR LEAST-SUCCESSFUL PEERS.

I spend a lot of time with middle-class parents who are puzzled and horrified that their teenagers have come to act like gangsters. It's a common pattern to see these days—teenagers who, for the most part, were "perfect" children before the ravages of hormones and rap music struck. Kids who formerly dreamed of being astronauts and archaeologists and professional athletes sometimes become surly pubescent barbarians whose lack of eye contact and distinct disinterest in developing a body of knowledge leave them hardly recognizable as themselves.

What most parents forget is by the time their girls are twelve and their boys are fourteen, they are a lot less interested in their parents' values than they are their peers' values. Those with the oppositional streak resist the middle-class values of their parents like all other kids. It's a normal developmental stage, but the oppositional child predictably takes it too far. The oppositional middle-class child looks at the lifestyle and behavior of the oppositional child from the decidedly non-middle-class home and sees everything he or she dreams about. No curfew. No rules. No concerned parent hovering in the background. The oppositional middle-class child is envious of the lack of rules and expectations in the homes of peers in which the structure has fallen apart and the children are allowed to run wild due to parental neglect, abuse, alcoholism, mental illness, and so on. They believe that because these children have no rules, demands, or expectations placed upon them, then neither should they.

To illustrate, we've all had this conversation: "Why do I have to be in by eleven?"

"Because that's when people your age are home on Friday night."

"Billy gets to stay out all night long if he wants to."

"You're not Billy, and I'm not Billy's mother."

Young Billy has this inordinate freedom because his family has fallen down around him and has failed him in many important ways. But your child does not have the cognitive complexity or mental and emotional maturity to see it this way. I jokingly tell parents all the time that all fourteen-year-old brains are faulty devices, in particular those of oppositional children. If they had reached the level of emotional maturity at which they could accurately think about the impact of their behavior on others, they would not be so surprised when all hell has broken loose at home because they started dressing and acting like gangsters. They seem to believe that because their friend Billy can act that way in his home, they can act that way in their own. The vast differences in the two settings fail to register with them.

Nevertheless, the oppositional, middle-class adolescent will attempt to knock down the rules and structure you have provided because he believes Billy's deal to be much better than the one afforded him by you. In the mind of the oppositional teenager, the attitudes and behaviors of the child from the fallen-down home look successful because they are so openly oppositional and defiant. Oppositional teenagers equate acting in a highly oppositional manner with success of some sort. Their highly oppositional peer is successfully showing the world that no one can make him do anything he doesn't want to do. Such behavior is often the envy of the budding oppositional child; it is what they strive to emulate.

There are several paradoxes here. The budding oppositional child from the middle-class family is typically unaware that the extreme attitudes and behaviors of the child from the fallen-down home are what will doom him to a pattern of failure in a society that values eye contact, manners, and complex answers to questions—answers that go far beyond the "I don't know" typically offered by oppositional teenagers.

The budding oppositional middle-class child is also typically unaware that his attitudes and behaviors often brand him as "stupid" or "loser" in the eyes of his nonoppositional middle-class counterparts and the middle-class adults he encounters. They seem to me shockingly innocent of the fact that their behavior and attitudes make others think of them as failed human beings. From their viewpoint, what they're doing is proving to the world that no one has power over them. To them this seems clearly necessary.

We live in an age where lots of children and teenagers equate oppositional behavior with success and coolness. I should mention, should it not already be clear, that the most highly oppositional teenagers are concerned primarily with their attitudes, their dress, and their peer groups. They don't seem to place being smart very high on the priority list.

I saw this a number of years ago while in a store near my office with one of my prepubescent oppositional patients. I had taken him there to buy him a soft drink as a reward for not getting in trouble the past week. There were two teenagers in front of us in line. Both wore tattered leather vests without shirts. Both had ill-formed, hand-made tattoos. On one boy's arm appeared to be the beginning of a girl's name: "Je". I assumed he chickened out because of the pain, and Jean, or whoever, never received full publicity on his forearm. Given the longevity of typical teenaged relationships, it was also possible that they broke up in the middle of the tattoo session.

When they got to the counter the clerk gave his usual friendly hello. Neither answered. Both threw their money on the counter. No eye contact, no acknowledgment of the clerk's existence. I asked my young client, who had been eyeing the tattoos, the metal studded belts, the bandanas tied around their legs just above their kneecaps, what he thought of these two.

"They're cool," he said.

RULE 10: OPPOSITIONAL CHILDREN AND TEENAGERS ATTEMPT TO ANSWER MOST QUESTIONS WITH "I DON'T KNOW."

This is another one of those rules that rings true with most parents when they hear me mention it. It's something they intuitively know, even if they hadn't yet put it into words. Teenage males are the worst. Ask an oppositional teenaged male a complex, but age-appropriate, question. Something on the order of "What kind of career are you thinking about having one day?" His head might tilt back, his eyes might glaze over. "I don't know," he'll say.

Oppositional children and teenagers often don't seem to like to think. To clarify this, they don't seem to like to think in ways that might be described as analytical unless they are arguing. When asked to simply swap information or opinions, they draw a blank. They seem to limit their thinking to topics such as how to gratify their immediate desires, what kind of tennis shoes are cool, what the hot rock or rap band is, and so on. Again, all of this is typical for teenagers. And again, the oppositional child and teen take it too far by totally ignoring our culture's demand that individuals build a knowledge base. To them, having the right attitude is sufficient.

However, this rule needs even further clarification in order to ring fully true. Oppositional children and teenagers do not like to be made to think by adults. The same teenager who answers all of your questions with numb silence may be a motor mouth with his peer group.

"I don't know" as an answer is at the root of intense conflict between many parents and their oppositional children. Many of the parents I see try to explain to their children that when they were in school it was better to die than to answer a question in class with "I don't know." To do so was a sign of being lazy at best, stupid at worst.

Not so with today's oppositional child. Answering with "I don't know" gives several subtle, unspoken messages. The first might be "Don't make me think." A second might be "I really don't know and am satisfied not to push on past my lack of knowledge." Third (and perhaps most important for oppositional teenagers), is that it's an invisible method of sticking up their middle fingers and waving them squarely in adults' faces in a manner that leaves adults unable to punish them. From the teenager's perspective, it wouldn't be fair to punish someone just because he didn't know the answer, would it?

RULE 11: OPPOSITIONAL LOGIC REVOLVES AROUND DENIAL OF RESPONSIBILITY.

Denying responsibility is, once again, typical of all teenagers. And, once again, oppositional children and teens take it too far. One teenage girl I know has an older brother whose pride and joy is his restored Mustang. Trying to be a good big brother, he let his sister drive it one night. She picked up some friends, and they eventually wound up drinking beer.

After several hours of driving and drinking, her friends were drunk, and two of them vomited in the car. The girl's brother got up the next morning to find his car soaked in vomit and confronted her about it. His sister, whom I know to be quite oppositional and defiant, responded that since it wasn't her who had thrown up, she wasn't about to clean it up.

I don't doubt that there are countless other "rules" about oppositional behavior, many more than I've been able to discover on my own. Oppositional children are constantly seeking to find the edge that allows them to do what they want, regardless of what their parents might expect or demand. You should expect them to be inventive in their logic, optimistic, and brave.

How do you handle such a child? We will try to find answers to that question in the following chapters. But first I will ask you to take a look at your family's structure.

CHAPTER TWO

The Importance of Structure

IF IT IS CLEAR to you that your child fits the behavior patterns and attitudes described in chapter 1, the next step is to learn how to control their oppositional and defiant behavior. After you accomplish this, you can help them change their thinking patterns and behavior. There is not a shortcut or straight road you can travel down quickly to achieve this outcome. Were this the case, parents could simply say to the opposition child, "I want you to change the way you act." However, it is my belief that all solutions for oppositional behavior begin by understanding the concept of structure.

STRUCTURE: BEFORE WE ASK A CHILD TO CHANGE, WE MUST LOOK TO OURSELVES

Am I saying that parents have to change? Listen for a second. All behavior occurs in a setting of some sort. This setting, or structure, is the atmosphere of expectations in the home, an atmosphere created by the parent or parents. It is all of the things involved in raising a child to be a healthy, happy, productive person. Structure is composed of rules, laws, rewards, punishments, love, guidance, sense of safety and security, and so on. Structure is what makes us feel safe and contained.

You should hope that I never invite you over to my house to watch my home movies. If you did come over, you might think I was a pretty poor cameraman, or you might wonder if I lived on a fault line. Many of my movies seem to bump about every ten seconds, almost like I was filming in the midst of a small earthquake.

Actually that small earthquake was my youngest son. From the time he first learned to walk to about age six, if I was standing up he was hanging on to my leg. He was seeking closeness, warmth, contact—all of which are part of structure. His constant bumping, moving, and jerking bounced me and my camera around, but his constant contact with me was making him feel safe. He knew where I was and had no doubt about my presence. This level of clarity makes for good structure.

Structure is best visualized as a corral, a large fence that encircles a child and reminds her on an ongoing basis of the acceptable limits of behavior. The nature of children is to challenge the limits imposed upon them by structure, to attempt to expand it or defeat it. You will rarely hear your child, oppositional or otherwise, say, "Mom, Dad, please give me a few more rules to follow."

The healthiest type of structure is a flexible one. Healthy structure closes in quickly around a child when she is doing poorly, the psychological equivalent of the calvary riding in to the rescue. But it expands when she is doing well and guarantees that she will have ample room to roam.

As a child psychologist I get the pleasure of watching many children finish high school and go off to college. I took particular interest in one young man a number of years back. He was a likable but goofy sort, the type of young man whose hair stuck out in places, whose glasses always seemed slightly askew, and whose pants always seemed just a tad too short. But of all the kids I watched go off to college that year, Joseph was the one I worried about the least. He had been going off to college campuses every summer for a number of years to attend various workshops for gifted and talented students, and his parents seemed to trust him implicitly. They trusted him to find his way around, to associate with reasonable peers, and to act in a reasonable manner. When I saw him at the end of his first semester he was on the Dean's list and appeared happy in all ways.

Joseph was raised in a home that employed flexible structure. When he was doing well, as was generally the case, he parents gave him few rules, set only a vague curfew, and did not have to spend much time telling him what was expected of him. When he was doing poorly, he found that his parents made exceptionally clear demands of his behavior, decreased his curfew time considerably, and made the rules quite explicit. When he was bad, the structure they created contracted and closed in around him. When he was good, they allowed it to expand. The flexibility of the structure allowed him to thrive, yet kept him feeling safe in uncertain times.

However, structure can be too contracted, too expanded, too flexible, or too rigid. Take the case of Jonathan. He was raised by a father who was a virulent drunk, the type of man who would be drunk on Saturday morning by the time his wife returned from grocery shopping and who would grab the new jar of apple juice and smash it against a wall. At his best he could be jocular and friendly, but given the nature of his drinking habit, his best was rarely in view. When drunk, he was dogmatic, authoritarian, inflexible, and he would allow his son to go nowhere. He preferred to have him there as a target to berate and abuse. It seemed entirely predictable that at some point his son would retaliate, and ultimately the retaliation mirrored the father's violent behavior. He beat his father to a pulp on several occasions once he turned eighteen.

Some children live in such contracted structures that they have to explode their way out of the house, and Jonathan was a case in point. But do not make the mistake of believing that it is just the abusive, negligent parent who sets such a stifling structure. Tom's mother, a well-educated but fearful single parent who had herself been raised by a tense, religiously fanatical mother, allowed her son little leeway to walk around his neighborhood, visit other boys at their homes, or go to football games. He had to carry tissue with him everywhere, out of her fear that he might get a nosebleed (not that he had them more often than his peers). She slathered him in suntan lotion and made him wear hats, for fear of skin cancer. Her fearfulness was contagious, and by the age of fourteen he had never tried roller skating, been sledding, or spent the night with a friend.

If we contrast Tom with Joseph we find two academically gifted young men, who, incidentally, went off to the same large undergraduate college. Joseph, as I said, made the Dean's list his first semester. Tom also made the Dean's list his first semester; then, unused to the relative lack of structure in the college environment, he promptly moved back home.

And then there are other children who live in structure so expanded that it is essentially porous. In this type of structure, anything goes. Parents and children get drunk or high together. No expectations exist. If the child doesn't come home and doesn't call, then no news is good news, as they say. No academic or social expectations are made. The parents who provide such loosely structured environments are often prone to say such things as "I just can't control him," in reference to their fifteen-year-olds. The level of control a parent is willing to exact is precisely what is different between a healthy, flexibly structured child-rearing environment and one with no structure at all.

Parents who establish a healthy structure around their children always assume they are in charge and are willing to defend the authority that accompanies their parental role in ways that are vigorous and rational. One of the marks of healthy structure is that the role of parent is not up for grabs. The child's attempt to defeat structure is met with tolerant, amused awareness that healthy children seek power. In situations in which tolerance and amused awareness do not work, such as with children whose drive to live outside the rules is so strong that they are immune to reason, logic, and gentle limit setting, then structure must be intensified accordingly. I have worked with any number of parents who tell me that they cannot ground their teenager because he or she will just leave the house. I point out that while the teenager is gone is the perfect time to go into his room and take everything of value—and I mean everything. The teenager returns to a room containing a mattress, a pillow, sheets, a blanket, one pair of basic jeans, two T-shirts, one jacket, one pair of shoes, a week's worth of underwear and socks, and nothing else. The parents who have gone this far tell me that by doing so they sent a strong message to their oppositional child: "I am in charge here. If you can't accept that, you will be very unhappy."

When structure is out of whack, children become symptomatic. Although problems in structure do not necessarily cause oppositional symptoms, symptoms always seem to be associated with breakdowns in structure. If this seems confusing, think of it this way: Cold weather does not cause snow, but the two are often associated.

It works like this: If you have a child who has a strong personality and who is prone to challenge rules and limits, problems in the structure are likely to make this trait worse. Certainly it seems to work the same way with other forms of psychopathology. If a child is anxiety prone, problems in the family structure will make it worse. It is the same with depression, the same with attention and learning problems, and so on. Improvements in family structure and functioning almost always help with these illnesses.

When structural problems are found in a family, they must be fixed before you can expect any behavior change of the child. This may strike some parents as an unnecessary extra step. Why not just impress upon the child that he must change? The answer is probably best illustrated in the example of young children who act violently toward their peers at school. There are a number of reasons for such behavior that may have relatively little to do with family structure. Children with attention problems who display hyperactive behavior quite often act in an impulsive, aggressive manner toward their peers in the first two years of school. Depressed children often strike out at their peers. Some children with what is known as a proprioceptive disorder are so literally touchy that they explode if others bump into them lightly or touch them unexpectedly. Some children who are unusually tense and anxious will strike out when things don't go as they expected. Others learn these attitudes from being treated like they are the center of the universe, which leads them to assume that they are the only important person on the face of the planet.

But regardless of the child's individual diagnosis, almost all of the children I see at my office who hit other children live in homes in which spanking and yelling are used as the main forms of punishment. As perverse as it may seem, parents tell me that they spank their children for hitting other kids at school, and they can't understand why they keep hitting other children. Such families provide prime examples of why family structure must be examined before a child can logically be expected to change.

Although the list of issues a family may need to examine about its own structure could be endless, it's important to center on several that are clearly related to the child's problematic behavior. Included are issues such as how well the parents get along, whether in marriage or in divorce; the mental health of the parents; parents' use and abuse of substances, and so on. Expectations of behavior change by the child should come only once the structure is examined and found to be solid or once problems in family structure are found and appropriate attempts to fix them are underway. Following are some suggestions parents can use when examining the structure they have created in their own homes.

EXAMINING THE PARENTAL RELATIONSHIP

I am presently seeing a couple whose daughter is in constant trouble at school, who seems to choose her boyfriends based on their ability to wreck her car, and who fits many of the defining characteristics of oppositional children. She assumes herself to be her parents' equal, argues with everything they say, rejects reason and logic, and lives with the fantasy of defeating all authority figures. She is bright but gets rotten grades. She argues daily with her teachers and has zero insight into her impact on others. She believes that people have it in for her.

The mother is a long-suffering sort of woman whom most people might describe as pleasant and sociable, and the father is a hard-nosed realist who believes that no one sees things quite as clearly as he. They are in the midst of a horrendous squabble over financial issues, have assumed separate bedrooms for the past year, and blatantly distrust each other's motives. They argue in my office about how to respond to their daughter's academic failure, her poor choice of friends, and the sexual risks she takes. I am fond of explaining that it takes two high-functioning adults to gang up on one oppositional teenager. Given that they mistrust each other and do not act as if they even like each other, they have no chance of constructing the sort of structure needed to reel their daughter in.

One of my favorite questions to parents like these is "When was the last time you had any fun?" I frequently watch them look puzzled for a moment, then they begin to search their memory banks. They often tell me they went to a movie six months ago, or out to dinner last year, or to the office Christmas party. They tell me that they have been so busy trying to contain their oppositional child that they don't find time for each other. I try to indicate to them clearly that, until they are functioning well as a couple, they have little chance of controlling an oppositional child. When marriage partners are unhappy or oppositional themselves, they will simply get in the way of each other in their attempts to deal with their child, only making the situation worse. It is important for them to get into couples counseling and repair their relationship before they can expect to control their oppositional child.

Why is couples counseling necessary when it is the child's behavior that is the problem? Children and teenagers are born geniuses when it comes to exploiting the rifts between parents. Every child has the drive to do so. When Mom tells daughter she can't have a popsicle, daughter will often head straight to dad. Examples such as this are handled easily enough if the parents are working together and have communicated to the kids that each parent speaks for the other. If mom says "We don't have popsicles before breakfast," it is the same as if dad has said it too.

But often this is not the case. I see children weekly whose parents are openly hostile toward each other or who say negative things about each other to their children. When parents are warring, children are unable to handle the ambiguity and uncertainty of the fight. Human beings don't like uncertainty because it frightens them. When children observe parents acting in an emotionally charged, unpredictable manner, they often do what movie directors do in order to make the situation understandable (remember, if we think we understand something, it seems less frightening): They assign the role of "good guy" to one parent, and the role of "bad guy" to the other parent. Here's the problem: You never can predict who they will put in which role. However, you can also bet that once a child believes that one parent is good and the other is bad, the one in the bad role will have a difficult time getting out of that role. Parents who want to avoid such role assignment must take their disagreements behind closed doors and take the high road with each other when around the kids.

Once children feel trapped between warring parents, they often become strategic themselves. It's easier to get permission to spend the week at the girlfriend's house who has the cute older brother when mom and dad are antagonizing each other than when they are working together. When parents work together, they're far more likely to tell their daughter that no one stays gone for a week at her age, to ask just who this girlfriend is and why they haven't met her, and to make clear that they don't really believe that her parents don't have a telephone number because of their religious beliefs.

Although it is true that not every child raised in the midst of warring parents will become oppositional, the lack of protective structure will allow whatever oppositional traits are there to expand and grow. I see two sisters presently, one sweet natured and quiet, the other with more of an "in your face" quality, the sort of girl who likes to play football with the neighborhood boys and delights in knocking them on their butts. The parents are going through a bitter, acrimonious divorce. The father, who visits seldom, tells the girls that their mother won't allow him to have visits because she doesn't want him to see them. The mother tells the girls their father doesn't want to see them. The sweet natured one continues to get good grades and perform well socially. The in-your-face one has become exaggeratedly so, to the point where she is often in trouble at home and increasingly in trouble at school. She explains to me that she is "like my dad. We're tough."

Bury the Ax, or Bury the Child

The ability to work together extends beyond the marriage relationship and into the divorce relationship. About half the kids I see at my office have divorced parents. Some of them tell me that almost all of their friends or classmates come from divorced families. The number of children I see from reconstituted families—parents who have divorced and remarried—also seems high. Some of these kids come from backgrounds in which the parents have divorced well, so to speak, and others come from families in which the parents have divorced badly. The difference in the child is often stunning. Children from careful divorces can remain relatively unaffected.

A case in point: Mike was sixteen and came to see me because his motivation to perform up to his ability in school was low. He had taken to skipping school with a few of his friends. He was as pleasant and friendly a young man as you would want to meet, with great social skills, friendly eye contact, a well-developed vocabulary, and so on. His father told me that all of his teachers liked him, believed in his potential, and were concerned about the recent negative turn in his grades and attendance.

Mike's background was interesting in that both of his parents were trial lawyers and both did a great deal of family law, a specialty in which you necessarily become involved in divorce and child custody litigation. You might well imagine that if there were two parents who would know how to rip each other's hearts out, it would have been Mike's. Instead, they chose to divorce in a style they hoped would have the least negative impact on their son.

They divorced when Mike was around age ten. They agreed that their son would remain with his mother in the house he had grown up in, and that they would work out an exceptionally liberal and flexible visitation schedule. As Mike hit his middle teenage years he was essentially able to spend equal time with each parent (other parents I know will take each other to court over being a half hour late returning a child from visitation). The father bought a house in the same neighborhood, only a few blocks away, so that when Mike was staying with him he would have no trouble getting to school. It also gave Mike the advantage of being able to simply walk over to his dad's house when he wanted to see him, or to his mom's house to see her when he was staying with his dad. He could continue to have contact with his own friends at either parent's home.

The parents had other interesting agreements. They agreed that if Mike's behavior had been terrible at his mother's, but it was his father's weekend to have visitation, then Mike would not go to his father's and proceed to enjoy himself. His father had canceled fishing trips because of negative behavior toward his mother, and he had been grounded from having friends come over to his mother's because of negative behavior toward his father. The parents did an excellent job of communicating with each other about his behavior and attitudes and gave him the clear message that even though they were divorced, they were still obligated to work together to raise him. He was not able to get away with a behavior pattern I see with lots of children from divorced families: Whack Mom with a ton of negative attitude on Friday night because you know that Dad will pick you up Saturday morning and not give a rip how you treated your mother.

Both parents attended the family counseling sessions with Mike. He was stubborn in his friendly way, insisting that it was his life and he should be able to do as he pleased. The message he got back from his parents was that if he made such poor choices, then he should expect them to work in concert to take away privileges such as money and free time. They guaranteed that his life would be quite boring and routine, given that he would go nowhere, have no access to telephones, televisions, cars, money, friends, the mall, and so on. He came around, over time, to their viewpoint.

I recall another child, about age six when I saw her a number of years ago. Her teachers had referred her to me, essentially wondering if she had some sort of thought disorder or if she was showing the initial signs of childhood schizophrenia.

She immediately attempted to take total control when we went into my office, telling me where to sit and proceeding to make up a game for us to play. The game made no sense at all, had no coherent rules, and was headed toward no conceivable end. She would grab a cup, then tell me to hold it and to give it a name. She would have me change seats. Then she might put paper clips in the cup, or go tap on my desk ten times. Then she would hide behind one of my chairs and pretend to sleep, after which she would teach me to say the ABCs. She did not allow me any input into the rules of the game and insisted that she had to be in charge. Sessions with her went that way for a number of weeks, and such was her disorganization that I also wondered if I wasn't dealing with a girl in the early stages of psychosis, something really quite rare in children.

Fortunately, as I continued to work with her the picture became more clear. The relationship between her parents was so volatile and oppositional that she had little chance of internalizing any real sense of peace, order, or structure. The games that she invented and controlled so rigorously taught me that she was attempting, like a little trooper, to create structure for herself because her parents failed miserably to make her feel safe.

Her father was the sort of man who bragged about all of the things he did to cause trouble for her mother, a depressed woman with a history of psychiatric hospitalization toward whom he held a remarkable grudge. He used to tell me when he talked about his schemes to create misery for her that she was going to "scream like a stuck pig." He bragged about some sort of financial manipulation that caused her to lose her house.

In the face of such things it becomes evident why a child would "act crazy." Children do not thrive in the absence of nurture and structure. The chaos and impulsivity that is inherent in the mind of a child who has been raised in a chaotic background begins to express itself outwardly because it is not being contained by the parents. When a child is left to create structure for herself because the parents are not emotionally available to do so, the result cannot resemble anything but the work of a child. Although horrifying, everyone who works in the court systems and the mental health systems has seen similar stories. The psychological chaos of the child we just talked about was the price of the animosity between her parents.

Other equally troubling results of divorce are commonly seen. For example, children caught between their parents often believe the parental conflict is their fault. If only they could become perfect, they imagine their parents will be happy and get back together again. I had one child tell me, "If I didn't sweat and make my clothes smell bad, my mom and dad would get back together." Children caught in the midst of parental conflict often assume it is their job to do something to solve the problems between the parents. I am currently seeing seeing a seven-year-old who believes that she should get on the phone and disguise her voice so that her father will think it is his wife. She will then have a conversation with him and solve the problems. Then everyone will be happy. She believes this is possible.

If you are divorced, look at the stories of the children we just discussed. If you are operating out of the same assumptions as Mike's parents—that cooperation where your child is concerned is paramount—then you are probably doing quite well when it comes to raising your children in a manner that keeps them psychologically healthy.

If the story of the child with the disorganized behavior reminds you of how you feel about your ex-spouse, then your child may be at extreme risk of being caught in the midst of parental conflict. You may wish to call your court system and ask who they consider to be the local experts for helping parents to solve problems related to their hostile feelings for each other. It is likely that someone there can give you the names of local therapists with expertise in your area. It is also possible that the court has a staff member who can meet with you to discuss your concerns. Although this varies from state to state, some courts have professional counselors on staff whose job is to provide counseling for warring parents.

If such resources are unavailable from your court system, look in the yellow pages to get names of local counselors, clinical social workers, and psychologists. Call a sampling and ask if they provide counseling or mediation for parents who are at odds with each other. If they don't, ask them for the names of associates who do. Once you find a therapist, get used to the idea that he or she may ask you to meet with your ex-spouse in an attempt to solve the issues. The first few meetings can be quite rough if you are in a situation in which both parents literally hate each other. Avoid having the meetings degenerate into a catalog of past grievances or attempts to find fault or place blame. Stay focused on the notion that you are both in the room to create a better situation for your child. Keep in mind that the best way to contain the oppositional child or adolescent is by having all of the adults in his life work with each other as cooperatively as possible.

PARENTS MUST EXAMINE THEIR OWN POTENTIAL FOR VIOLENCE

Among the hardest of the self-interrogations parents have to face when examining family structure is to ask whether they keep their child safe. One of the most (literally) tortured children I have met was a twelve-year-old I'll call Domingo. His mother had broken both of his elbows with a pipe, and due to this, when he walked his arms were cocked out to the side. The sad outcome was that his stance gave him the look of the classic tough guy, and he was constantly getting challenged to fight by real tough guys.

Such overt physical abuse is not the only sort of violence parents should be wary of, however. We continue to live in a culture that holds on to the belief that hitting children is somehow of benefit to them. Hitting children scares them. When most parents hit, their faces are red with anger and they look ten times larger because they are moving with speed and angry intent. If you want your child to be afraid of you and to harbor private fantasies of defeating you, hitting them is the perfect device to this end.

Many parents are in truth afraid to seek counseling for their violent tendencies because they fear being turned in to authorities who will remove their children from their home. If you are secretly violent and brutal to your child, it may very well be in his best interest to be allowed to live elsewhere until you have successfully changed your beliefs and behavior so that you no longer pose a danger to him. To voluntarily ask your state to assume guardianship of your child while you undergo therapy is a touchy issue. I typically suggest that people who are considering this option consult an attorney to be clearly apprised of the law in their state. I do, however, know of a number of individuals who have done precisely this, and the courts have been relatively cooperative in working with them. Judges, in general, have no desire to permanently remove children from parents who are making an honest effort to change.

If you are not brutal or violent but believe that you depend too much on yelling or spanking, you may wish to contact a therapist who can discuss parenting skills training with you. Like many therapists, I find that parents who rely on yelling and spanking often admit that they just don't know what other techniques to employ. Most child therapists can help round out your repertoire of options so that you will have other techniques to turn to.

You Cannot Be Alcohol or Drug Dependent and Function Fully as a Parent

This is where I'm guaranteed to offend or hurt, so allow me to apologize in advance. That said, I believe that you cannot maintain your involvement with drugs and alcohol and at the same time maintain your involvement with your child. The two are mutually exclusive. For example, I was talking to a mother recently, a woman who is in substance-abuse recovery and who is about six months along in a twelve-step program. She is to be congratulated for attempting to heal herself of addiction, but she remains so obsessed with it that I can't get her to stop talking about herself long enough to talk about her children. The point here is that addicts become obsessed with their addictions and often can see nothing else.

There is a pattern I see over and over with the adults I work with who were raised in alcohol- or drug-rich environments. In some unconscious way they realized at an early point, typically around the first grade, that they were not getting the attention and affection from the addicted parent that they needed. Being children, and analyzing the world with the childish idea that everything in their family is somehow caused by them, they come to the (again, unconscious) conclusion that if they were "good enough," the addicted parent would notice them and be more nurturing. So, they do one of two things: they either quit trying, or they set out to get the attention they need by overachieving.

The ones who attempt to overachieve probably don't become highly oppositional (they probably become depressed because they will never be able to get the attention of the addicted parent). The ones who quit trying often have to defend themselves from teachers and parents by being oppositional. It helps to remember that it is unlikely that these children wanted to stop trying or stopped for no reason at all. It is also important to keep in mind that they probably don't like themselves at all and have little faith in their own abilities.

The teenagers I work with who have addicted parents tell me over and over that they doubt their self-worth and their abilities, and far too often the precipitating event that brings them to my office is a crisis in self-concept. Sometimes they feel suicidal, but they don't know why. They can't point to any one event that has brought them down. All they know is that they don't like themselves, and they see dying as a way to make the pain stop.

Oppositional children are difficult enough for sober parents to contend with. Asking yourself to deal with one while you are intoxicated or high is expecting the impossible. Plus, there is the question of what addicted behavior teaches the oppositional child about adults in general. Remember, oppositional children have a marked tendency not to trust adults. Presenting yourself to them in a drunken or diminished capacity only reinforces the notion that adults aren't worth listening to anyway. You can't expect your child to respect and obey you if you're not holding up your end of the bargain by providing a stable structure in which your attention is focused on your child, not your addiction.

IF YOU DON'T NURTURE YOUR TEENAGER, SOMEBODY ELSE WILL

Suzie was a perfectly normal thirteen-year-old from an upper-middle-class family. Until the months before I saw her, she had gotten reasonably good grades and had developed long-term friendships with girls from families with similar middle-class expectations of their children. Unfortunately, Suzie's father's version of being nurturing was to warn her that one more doughnut would make her "butt look like a blimp." Whether true or not, she believes that he likes nothing about her and has no respect for her. She was dying for a nurturing male to come into her life, and unfortunately he arrived in the form of a seventeen-year-old dropout with a criminal record. He tells her he loves her. These words are balm to her soul.

I hope at this point you are beginning to think about the structure you have created for your own child. Children with ODD need firm, clear structure. It should be flexible, giving them plenty of room to roam when they are doing well, but it should contract around them when they are not doing well. You must take into consideration the manner in which they are not doing well because it will guide you in what to do. If your child seems mired in self-hatred and no longer wants to go anywhere or do anything, he is probably depressed and needs a structure leading to treatment, not punishment. If your child is not doing well because she runs with the wrong crowd, alienates every adult she comes into contact with, and keeps your house in an uproar, the structure should also include treatment. However, it should also squeeze her in ways that leave it clear that you will begin to withhold all of the goodies that she has daily access to until she begins to live in a more reasonable manner. There are certain beliefs and attitudes that parents need to embrace before they can win this particular battle, however. We will examine these next.

| CHAPTER THREE |

Necessary Ideas

I OFTEN ASK MYSELF what separates parents who have a relatively easy time dealing with their defiant children from parents who have a relatively hard time (I stress the word "relatively"—no defiant child is easy to parent). The difference seems to lie in attitudes about the parental role itself. The more successful parents conceive of their roles differently than those who are struggling. Fortunately, the ideas, attitudes, and beliefs of successful parents can be learned. They are presented below, with the suggestion that they are essential to successfully raising an oppositional, defiant child and maintaining your own sanity.

You Can't Take It Personally

Many parents tell me they have failed. Their proof of failure is their child's behavior. I certainly believe that parents make many mistakes, and this is why I have gone to great lengths so far to ask parents to look at the structures of their families. However, one point that I stress with parents is that children have personalities, and oppositional personality traits are sometimes just part of who the child is. Academic psychologists write entire books on the nature of personality and the extent to which it is genetic versus learned. Suffice it to say at this point that nature and nurture seem to work together. A child comes into the world with certain traits, and these interact with and become modified by the environment.

I have met children who have been oppositional and defiant seemingly since birth. One boy I work with is three and a half years old and has already been kicked out of several day care facilities because he constantly argues with teachers. He bullies, hits, and pushes the other children, grabs their toys, and seems impervious to the punishments that the day care providers mete out (typically they use time out or separation from the group). He is very bright, vigorous, and relentless. He's happy as a clam as long as he is getting his way. His grandmother, who has custody of him, and another lady who has been his baby-sitter at times, both tell me he has always been this way.

Oppositional behavior is sometimes even more upsetting to parents whose children were not defiant at an early age. These are the parents of the "model" child who has recently become the monstrous terror from the movies. The story here is usually that these children watch their peers get away with outrageous behavior at school, on the playground, or in the community and decide that they will try it out for themselves. We should not fail to remember that we live in an age in which it is more "cool" than ever to openly defy authority. In fact, I would guess that twenty years ago most adults would have looked at predictions of guns in high schools, drugs in elementary schools, popular music infused with the most vile words imaginable, and nine-years-olds with the vocabularies of dock workers as being a bad fantasy from some apocalyptic science fiction tale.

The point I'm leading to is this: Although it is certainly possible to raise a child in a poor enough fashion to make them oppositional and defiant, most of the ones I see in my practice either have these traits as part of their personality or they have been influenced by their peer culture and have begun to emulate their oppositional mentors. Only a few of the ones I know are completely the inventions of their parents' poor practices. Parents need to conclude at some point that it is a waste of time to sit and wonder where they went wrong. The necessary move is to examine the family structure and fix what needs fixing, then begin to make new demands on the oppositional child to change his behavior.

I'm the Parent, You're the Child

Part of developing your battle plan is to stop and get a sense of who all the players in the game really are. It helps here to consider the notion of power. Children and teenagers do indeed have a lot of power, but it is power of the emotional sort. Only a very small percentage of them can act in a manner that is dangerous. For the most part, their power is limited to their ability to bug, irritate, make angry, and disappoint.

Parents, on the other hand, have power of a legal sort. As long as they act in a manner that is rational, consistent, and not abusive, the legal power they have over a child or teenager is close to absolute. The problem is that most parents forget this along the way. They get down in the trenches with their oppositional children and engage in a battle fought from the emotional viewpoint of the child, not from the legal viewpoint of the adult. The real difficulty in parenting the oppositional child comes when the parent lowers his or her standard of behavior to that of the child.

Look at a typical example of this: Your daughter who used to be well socialized and academically talented but who has recently taken to hanging out with bleary-eyed oppozoids tells you she wants to go to a party at a friend's house tonight and intends to spend the night. You ask if the party is being supervised and who is going to be there. She tells you that you're trying to treat her like a baby because she is, after all, "like fifteen," and tells you that she is going whether you like it or not. You tell her that you don't like it, that she's not going, and that if she tries to go you won't let her out the door. She begins to scream even more about how everyone she knows is treated better and says she will call her friends to come get her. You begin to scream about all of your hard work and everything you've given her, and soon the volume is turned up to ten. She threatens to report you for child abuse for yelling at her and barring the door, and you threaten to nail her windows shut and ground her until she's old enough to draw social security.

In situations like this it is crucial to take the attitude that you are the parent and your role is not up for grabs. It is also important to remain strategic and to begin analyzing the thinking errors your daughter is engaging in at the time of the argument. If you recall the rules in chapter 1, she is certainly engaged in the fantasy of defeating the adult. She is also ignoring your wishes, believing you will finally cave in and tell her to just go. She is attempting to assume the position of your equal in this struggle. Chances are she's seen her new friends act this way with the teachers at school or heard them brag about treating their parents this way.

At this stage of conflict it is not so important what you do as what you don't do. Do not allow yourself to be pulled into a yelling match. Yelling matches are teenagers' turf. They will win every one of these contests because they believe they have nothing to lose. Everything they say will only shock or hurt you more once you engage in the yelling, and you will come out bruised. Your better choice is to remain parental. You say, "I'm sorry. But if you can't tell me who is going to be there and who is going to supervise, then I won't allow you to go. This is not something I am willing to argue with you about."

Your teenager, at this point, has two choices. She can back down, perhaps muttering under her breath as she does, or she can escalate. Should she choose to escalate, you must then stay calm and indicate that as the parent you have already given your answer. Should she be able to convince you that the party is adequately supervised, which you will verify, and should she be able to convince you that the people attending are people you will allow her to be around, then she may go. Otherwise, you say, you feel little need to repeat yourself.

That last part was actually a lie. Your strategy here is to repeat yourself, calmly, for as long as it takes. Your daughter may begin to escalate, may even go into full-blown nuclear hissy fit, but if you stick tightly to your calm, parental role, you cannot be defeated. Remember, you can only be defeated when you move out of the parental role and begin to argue like a teenager.

I have many parents take me to task on this before they try it. What if, they ask, your daughter says that there is no way you can keep her at home and that if you get in her way she will hit you, shove you away, or climb out a window?

Parents should tell the teenager two things at this point. Step one: Tell her you have no intention of doing something so stupid and juvenile as standing in front of a door or trying to keep someone from escaping. That would be acting like a teenager. Her decision to follow your rules or to ignore them is entirely her own. You indicate that if she leaves when you have said not to, she will return to a wasteland. Her room will be stripped to the bare walls. Everything of value will be taken out, and once taken, it might not return. If it returns, it will return only a few objects at a time, based entirely on her good behavior. If she insists on acting this way, she can say good-bye to whatever else you provide as well, such as telephone,

TV, transportation, money, trips to the mall, make-up, having friends over, access to snacks, ability to go into the fridge and get drinks on demand, ability to take long baths and showers, and so on.

Step two: Tell her that if she ever makes the mistake of hitting you, you will call the police and press charges against her. Inform her that although she will probably not go to jail for such an offense (unless she has a prior history of assaultive behavior), she certainly will be placed on probation and will have to meet with a probation officer weekly. She will probably be sentenced to a number of hours of community service. Insist that she pay the court costs, which will be substantial. If the judge orders her into counseling, you will insist that she pay a portion of its cost as well. Then inform her that after all of this, you will still do everything you threatened to do in step one. Say all of this in a calm, parental manner, and then follow through so she doesn't perceive you as a liar.

It is equally important—and equally parental—to praise your daughter for making a smart decision should she choose to back down or should she choose to give you the information you need to make your decision. In such a situation you let your child know that she is acting in a mature manner and that by doing so you are much more prone to trust her and to allow her to use her own judgment. Although you may not allow her to go to this particular party, such mature behavior on her part will ensure that she gets to make many of her own choices in the future.

PARENTS OWN EVERYTHING IN THE HOUSE

I alluded to this point above, but now is time to make it more explicit. It is my practice to explain to parents and children that parents own everything. The typical oppositional child or teenager will respond with something like this: "You can't take away my bike (substitute TV, stereo, phone, car, whatever). That's mine and I can use it when I want to."

I go to some lengths to point out that, in fact, children under the age of majority cannot legally own anything, even those things they have purchased with their own money. And they have no legal claim on the objects in the house that are typically for family use but paid for by the parents.

The list of things most children who grow up in the so-called middle-class home have available to them is truly staggering. I ask parents to make a list in my office, with their child or teenager participating (usually grudgingly so). I suggest that they make a list of what I refer to as "obvious reinforcers" and "subtle reinforcers." The obvious reinforcers are, well, obvious. They include such things as family and individual televisions; stereos; CD players; headphones; video players; computers; computer games; telephones; bicycles; skateboards; transportation such as cars, bikes, and motorcycles; fishing equipment; sports equipment; money; ability to have friends over or to go visit friends; access to public facilities such as malls, theaters, bowling alleys, skating rinks, and so on. The subtle reinforcers are things parents rarely think of controlling, but they make a huge impact on kids when they are actually controlled. These include such things as the ability to take a long shower or bath, access to cool T-shirts, shorts, jeans, or jackets (while grounded they lose access to any clothing item with designer labels, sports teams, music groups, or other logos, and have to wear their "generics"). Depending on the circumstances, you can also include access to snacks and drinks, the right to have pictures and posters on the walls of their rooms, access to collected items (sports cards, coin collections, model cars and planes), ability to have a part-time job, and so on. It is important for the parent to let the child or teenager know that all of these things, both subtle and obvious, are accessed through the parent.

PARENTS SET THE STANDARDS FOR THE FAMILY

If you have a teenager, chances are at least once they have brought home a friend who dressed and acted strangely or who answered every question with a grunt. For the prepubescent set it is essentially the same. My fifth grade son goes to school with a girl who has a pierced navel, for example. Given that kids and teenagers live by a sort of mob mentality, if one kid shows up at school wearing his underwear on the outside of his pants and is deemed cool for doing so, then within five days fifty kids will be dressed like him.

I saw a wonderful example of this many years ago while serving as an intern in a St. Louis hospital. Our girls unit, which housed girls of ages thirteen to seventeen, was operating with no major problems. Then the new girl rode in. She was from out West, with a gunslinger attitude. She dressed in a manner of particular note: heavy eye make-up, a long-sleeved white shirt several sizes too large (this was many years before the current fad of baggy clothes), and mound of necklaces around her neck. They were of various lengths and thicknesses. Some were simple chains, others held pendants, still others held charms. There had to have been at least fifty of them.

Within two days the second most powerful girl in the group (the new girl took all of about ten seconds to establish dominance) was dressed just the same, although it never became quite clear where she got all of the necklaces. By the end of a week all but the most unpopular girls had adopted the look. In addition to the look, they had adopted the walk, the talk, and the attitude. Soon enough the unit was in turmoil.

Families are this way. You son or daughter encounters someone with a new look or attitude, brings it home, and something about it just won't do. Your position is that the look and attitude are unacceptable. Their take on it is that it is their life, so buzz off.

You have to be careful here. There is nothing good about turning our children into clones of ourselves. At the same time it seems unwise to allow them to deviate far beyond cultural norms. True, some teenagers have tattoos, but most don't. Some dress in all black and write suicidal poetry. But most don't.

What are these cultural norms? At the risk of oversimplifying, in my office I see more similarity in values than dissimilarity between parents of varying ethnic and socioeconomic groups. Most parents I work with expect their children and teenagers to act in a polite manner, work up to their potential, and respect the rights of others. The parents who come to my office are very disturbed when their children deviate from these core values.

Parents have the obligation to insist that children leave the nest with a certain set of skills, such as the ability to read and write well, maintain a conversation, engage in critical reasoning, and conduct themselves in a way that poses no risk or annoyance to others. These attributes are important because of their potential to help children become successful in life. It's safe to allow a child or teenager to express his individuality as long as he exhibits the positive attributes mentioned above and doesn't go totally out in left field in his manner of expression. It's also reasonable to go into red alert when you see your child begin to reject these core values and gravitate toward a lifestyle that creates risk, whether the risk is something as poten-tially innocuous as developing bad habits or as potentially harmful as early addiction or violence.

Parents should always ask about hair, dress, and music. The basic rules should be to not get upset if your child or teenager stays somewhere in the middle of his range of peers. By peers, I do not mean only his immediate friends but also the full range of people he goes to school with. Your high schoolers go to school with a diverse group. Spend some time at your child's school. If the way your child wears his hair and the way he dresses are on the extreme of the range, then something may be wrong. I worry as much about eight-year-olds in gray three-piece suits and MBA haircuts as I do about eight-year-olds with pierced nostrils.

As for music, I've found that any quality music store will allow you to open any tape or CD you wish so that you can read the words to the songs. You should do this; you will be surprised at the lyrics. There are no groups who cater to preteens, so preteens tend to listen to the same groups that seventeen-year-olds listen to. The lyrics of many of the most popular groups are questionable enough for teenagers and totally inappropriate for preteens.

PARENTS MUST REMAIN IN CONTROL OF THEMSELVES

When parents frequently yell, shout, threaten, or strike out physically while angry, they send a profound message: No one is in control. The effect this has on a child is something akin to being a passenger in an airplane who looks in the cockpit and finds the pilot and copilot punching each other out. Who's flying the plane?!

If parents frequently engage in outbursts, the children get the message over and over that no one is flying the plane, so to speak. Any smart child will attempt to bail out. Children bail out in a number of ways. The young ones, in particular, become depressed. They believe that the family tension is their fault, and they begin to think of themselves as bad kids. Teenagers tend to take one of several roads. They act out their anger about what is going on at home toward teachers, adult strangers, or peers. They might turn to drugs to soothe themselves, or to alcohol, or to food, or to sex. They get involved in quasi-marital relationships by age fifteen in an attempt to make new families for themselves. There are hundreds of other reasons kids try to bail out. However, parents who do not maintain control of themselves are the ushers who most clearly point the way toward the exit.

Parents Cannot Be Held Hostage by Threats

I worked with a woman a number of years ago whose husband would threaten to kill himself whenever they got into an argument or whenever he couldn't get his way. When I met her she was worried, anxious, and guilty because she didn't want to remain in her marriage but didn't want her husband's blood on her hands. These were my instructions: The next time he threatened to kill himself she was to inform him that she intended to dial 911 and tell the emergency operator that her husband was about to take his life. She was to tell him that she could not allow him to harm himself and assure him that she would do everything possible to see that he was taken to a psychiatric hospital and given the best of care for his mental illness. I instructed her to say all of this with a straight face and in a realistic manner.

At our next session she told me that she had done exactly as I had suggested and that it had stopped her husband's threats in their tracks. She also learned that he thought she liked it when he acted that vulnerable. She explained to him that she did not like it at all, that it made her feel manipulated and resentful.

I have extended this same technique to families. I ask families to take their children's threats very seriously. If a child or teenager threatens to kill herself, the best move the parent can make is to get her to their physician or counselor as quickly as possible. It does not matter if it is just a ploy or an attempt to manipulate. Such a strong response on the part of the parent shows beyond a doubt that the parent is in charge and will do whatever is necessary. This tightens the structure around the child. She may kick against it, but it will make her feel safer and more contained. The result is that if she was truly entertaining suicidal thoughts, she would get to talk about it with a trained professional. If she was just trying to jerk you around, then she would also get to talk about it with a trained professional. I suggest to parents that they use this response to all serious threats, such as threats to harm others, threats to harm the parents, or threats to run away.

HUMOR IS MORE POWERFUL THAN MUSCLE

Oppositional children and teenagers expect you to approach them with hostility. Their entire set of defenses is tuned to seek and find indications of hostility in adults, something like a radio receiver tuned to pick up only one station. They don't respond well when someone interacts with them in a friendly or humorous manner. Often their response is to increase their own hostility or oppositionality in a manner that will make you angry. Once you are angry, they know how to respond because they are on familiar ground.

The main way oppositional children and teenagers make strangers (particularly psychologists) aware of their anger and resistance is by refusing to look at them. This is more common among males than among females. For both sexes the second line of defense is to answer your initial question to them by looking away and mumbling "I don't know."

It is at this exact juncture, just after you have met them and just when you are trying to pry the first answer out of them, that they expect to make you angry at them. They assume, at some level, that ignoring you and answering your questions with a refusal even to consider your questions will make you mad. Then the game can begin. Ask yourself how many times you have set out to pry an answer out of your oppositional child or teenager only to end up enraged, in an argument, and nowhere close to the answer you wanted.

It is much better at this point to lead with humor, not with muscle. Here is an example of a fairly typical interaction I might have with a sixteen-year-old oppositional male.

"How did you do in school this past semester?"

His head tilts back, his mouth falls open, his eyes glaze over. "I don't know," he finally mumbles.

"Do you know what 'I don't know' really means?"

"I don't know."

"The purpose of the brain is to know stuff. You brain makes two watts of electricity, that's how it works. When someone says 'I don't know,' what they're really saying is 'My brain is not engaged because I'm conserving electricity.' "

It's right about at this point that they think they have me. Usually they say "So?" Sometimes they say nothing, just stare blankly.

This is when I turn to his parents and explain humorously that we may have a crisis on our hands. If someone's brain is disengaged, I say, it would be dangerous to allow them to operate complicated devices. By complicated devices, I'm talking about televisions, stereos, CD players, remote controls, telephones, automobiles, and the like. They might break these things, or they could hurt themselves. If someone's brain is not engaged, I say, it would also be foolish to allow them to leave the house alone. They might get lost.

The payoff of humor, if you use it well, is that your teenager learns that you will acknowledge his behavior without anger and respond to it in a way that will not hurt. Teenagers are not old enough or subtle enough to defy you without trying to hurt you, but they like and respect adults who have this ability. Many of my oppositional teens, once they get to know me and let down their guard a bit, will try to answer me with "I don't know," then smile sheepishly, put their hand over their mouths, and say "Oops!" I use it as a constant source of teasing with them. "There you go," I'll say. "Conserving electricity again."

This is where it is very important for the parent to do a bit of real self-examination about how they interact with their oppositional child or teen. If your use of humor strikes others as a veiled attempt to shame the child or induce guilt in the child, then do not expect it to work. At the same time, if your secret thinking is something along the line of "I'm not going to let that little @#&* get the best of me," then chances are you will walk away frustrated every time. It becomes important to see in a humane way the humor in the oppositional child's attempt to control adults. He is doomed to fail because, after all is said and done, he can't use your car without your keys and he can't slam his bedroom door if you take it off the hinges and put it in the basement for a few days. Oppositional children are geniuses at getting you mad. But in truth, they are just children floundering around in an attempt to become powerful. It is much better to enjoy their attempts and approach them with a sense of humor than to take it personally.

In a very serious way, your child's ability to accept and deal with humor directed toward him can be diagnostic. I have met many oppositional children who have a sense of humor, even when the joke is on them. On the other hand, I have never met a young sociopath with a sense of humor. About the only time you will see a sociopath laugh is when he has hurt someone, wounded them deeply. Sociopaths have absolutely no sense of humor about themselves and will quickly resort to physical altercations when they are on the receiving end of a joke. I am not saying that your child is a sociopath if he does not respond well to your attempts at humor. He may be defending himself against something in your manner that suggests a veiled attack or an attempt to induce guilt or shame, or he may be anxious or depressed. With the child who never exhibits a sense of humor, however, there is cause for serious concern.

Anxious children and teenagers also seem to have little intact humor. They are too busy worrying to see the fun in things, so jokes often go right over their head. It would be rare to see them become violent, though. If anything, your joke might hurt their feelings, or they might worry that they didn't get the right meaning out of it.

Children and teenagers who are depressed or who suffer from chronic poor self-concept also do not respond well to humor. To them it feels like an attack. To be more precise, it feels like just one more attack in a life of attacks. At the same time, they are dying to be part of the group. Save your humor for them until after you do the more important work of helping them heal their self-hatred.

A Child's Attempt to Gain Power Is Healthy

I've alluded to this point several times, but it seems important to formally include it in the list of necessary ideas. Children gain power just like they gain space. When a six-month-old crawls around the corner out of the sight of her mother, it is an important developmental event. It means that the child has internalized a sense of the mother that she carries with her. She no longer has to have her mother in sight to be assured she still exists. When your child begins to challenge your rules and regulations, it is the emotional equivalent to going around the corner. She is beginning to believe that she can operate independently, that she can proceed without you and your guidance.

Some children make the grab for power in a clumsy manner; some do it so well you hardly even notice. Keep in mind that it is the style of the oppositional child to (as in all other things) go overboard in their attempt to gain power. Although the normal child will whine or complain or mutter under her breath, or simply stomp away, the oppositional preteen might pitch a full-blown temper tantrum, slam doors until their hinges loosen, or threaten to go live with a friend because you won't let her do what she wants.

The oppositional teenager will often be like the oppositional child, only more so. Oppositional teens seem fond of punching holes in their bedroom walls. I knew one family that spent more than $1,300 having the walls in their house patched and repainted because every time the parents came into conflict with their sixteen-year-old son, he would put his fist through the dry wall.

Although painful, it becomes important to see these situations for what they are: The child or teenager is revealing his belief that power must be wrenched out of the hands of adults. The oppositional child never stops to consider that power can be negotiated or earned. Perhaps if the skinny twelve-year-old in a muscle shirt who stands defiantly on the corner smoking a cigarette realized how truly ridiculous he looked, he would quickly find another way to get power. Perhaps the thirteen-year-old who uses too much eye make-up and jewelry is not aware that she looks cheap and sleazy. In her internal world, she is a model, a sophisticate.

Children need to consistently heighten their sense of themselves as powerful beings. It's important to give them healthy ways to do so. Reward them with extra freedoms when they handle their lives well. Let them make more of their own decisions once it is clear that they try hard to make good decisions. No sane parent wants to produce a powerless child. Understanding that it's not the oppositional child's drive for power that is problematic but the strategies he's using to obtain it can help you maintain a positive attitude about an endlessly frustrating situation.

You Must Be Willing to Make Your Child Miserable

I sometimes hesitate when I hear myself telling the parents of an oppositional child that they must be willing to make their child miserable. I don't want to sound harsh or mean. I am certain, however, that oppositional children have an innate ability to ignore reason and logic. If you simply talk at them, even yell at them, it has little impact. When an oppositional child believes he can defeat his parents, then his parents must be willing to devote themselves to proving that they are willing to make him unhappy.

Parents often counter with "But if I'm spending all of my free time making him unhappy, won't I be making myself unhappy too?" The answer is yes, of course you will be unhappy during the process. But what are the alternatives? If you do not counter your child's oppositional behavior with strong medicine, he will get the message that what he is doing is just fine and will continue along his oppositional way.

Although I joke with parents that they have to spend all their free time making their child miserable, the truth of it is that the misery-making process usually has to go on for only a few days, in most cases, to get the child's complete attention. Usually the parents have to administer a second dose of misery several weeks after the first dose—as we've already said, oppositional children are optimistic. Yours will probably believe that you won't be willing to go through the misery-making more than once yourself.

How do you go about making a child miserable? When is this an option? I will go into techniques in some depth in a later chapter, but let's take a look at the example of Dennis. He is eleven, very bright, very strong willed, and very manipulative. He tends to reserve most of his highly oppositional behavior for the times that his father is out of town on business. He warned his mother before they brought him to see me that if she tried to punish him, he would just do more bad things. He will do things such as lock himself in the bathroom and flush the toilet over and over or kick on the door to make noise. He will stand at his mother's bedroom door in the evenings and say "Mom" over and over. When his mother answers he just says "Mom" again. If she closes her door, he will stand and knock on it. He knows it drives her nuts. He argues constantly and keeps things stirred up with his siblings. His parents typically go to bed exhausted, and his siblings complain that their lives are miserable because of all of the fighting and arguing that goes on around them. He wrecks every trip and outing, and his need for constant attention leaves his parents feeling like they have not paid any attention to the other kids. The other children end up semi-raising themselves while he absorbs all the parental energy. Because he sucks up all the energy around him, his parents sometimes refer to him as the Black Hole.

When I first met Dennis I explained to him that I was aware that he had warned his mother that if she tried to punish him, he would only do more bad things. He beamed and nodded that it was true, he would.

The very first step in making a child miserable is to surprise them, to throw them off of their game plan. Dennis thought I would launch into some sort of lecture and had previously told his parents that he didn't have any intention of listening to anything that some stupid psychologist had to say. Instead of lecturing him, I thanked him for his willingness to do lots of bad things.

I said I would be teaching his parents lots of new ways to make him unhappy when his behavior was defiant. I explained that his behavior was making them unhappy, and all of their attempts to talk him into new ways of acting had failed. Due to this, the only thing left was for his parents to make him unhappy until he decided to change. I said that his willingness to do lots of bad things would give his parents many opportunities to practice their new punishments. I thanked him for being so willing to help his parents master their new techniques and explained to him that, of course, they could not practice these new techniques unless he was doing bad things. This is the second rule of making a child miserable—always give them an out. Some children will hear my explanation, like the one above, and decide that they don't want to challenge the parents to prove their willingness to make them miserable. If they have an out, quite often they will try to make changes immediately. But given the nature of oppositionality, lots of kids think you're just kidding.

Dennis wanted to know what kind of things I was going to teach his parents to do. I explained to him that I had about a hundred things I teach parents to do and would tell him one. The next time he did something outrageous like lock himself in the bathroom and begin to flush the toilet, instead of yelling at him, threatening him, or trying to use reason and logic, they were simply to act as if nothing had happened. The next day they were to put everything he owned in boxes.

Dennis began to argue with me before I could finish. "That wouldn't be fair," he said.

He then declared that if they did anything to his stuff, he would do the same thing to them.

You should not be surprised to hear oppositional children use this line of logic. This is part of their belief that they are equal to their parents. I began to explain to him that he might be making a mistake by doing to his parents what they were going to do to him. I explained that because he was a kid, he did not own anything. That, in fact, his parents owned everything. They could even go so far as to give away things that he had bought with his own money if he decided to push the issue of equality. I explained that his parents would be quite willing to prove to him that he was not their equal. If it took taking away everything he owned, then they would do it. I asked him to let me finish describing what his parents were going to do with the boxes of his stuff. If he continued to make them as unhappy as he had recently, then they would tell him that he no longer had free access to anything. He would have to check out underwear and socks, pants, shirts, and shoes on a daily basis the way one checks out a book from the library. They would be the librarians for all of his goods, only they would make the decision on what he could check out. He would not be guaranteed access just because he wanted to check out his headphones, for example. I assured him he would not like this arrangement. I let him know that these were just the techniques his parents would use to begin with, and that if these didn't work, they would be willing to try many, many more. I reiterated that, of course, his parents would not be able to use these techniques if his behavior was good, because it would not be fair to punish him for being good. I told him I knew for a fact that once his behavior changed, instead of his parents having to do crazy things like I had just described to him, they would be able to praise him and have fun with him again.

Just as I suspect that there are many "rules" about the behavior and beliefs of oppositional children that I have failed to state, I also doubt that I have come close to stating all of the "necessary ideas" for parenting the children with ODD. Hopefully the ideas covered above will at least help you begin to clarify your thinking about your own parenting strategies.

After you have begun to outline your new methods, it will be necessary to talk with your oppositional child or teenager about the punishments they should expect for negative behavior and the rewards they can expect for positive behavior. These issues are explained in the next chapter.

CHAPTER FOUR

Talking to an Oppositional Child or Teenager

IN CHAPTER 1, you learned how oppositional children and teenagers think. Your knowledge of this is important in talking with them, both so that you understand how they see the world and so you don't fall into arguing with them. In chapter 2 you learned how to examine your home environment to see if there are reasons your child acts in an oppositional manner, reasons that you can remedy. Chapter 3 presented some of the necessary ideas and attitudes needed to deal with oppositional children. If you have reviewed and thought about all of this, you're ready to put together your strategy for talking with your child.

Talking to your child or teenager about their behavior is always the first place to start in your attempt to regain control of the situation. If you move too quickly to punishment, it can create lasting resentment for both you and your child. Each of you will remember the other as someone who was impossible to talk to. Interactions with oppositional children must be based on a strategy, otherwise you will be pulled into arguing and fighting and nothing will get resolved. This is why we have to look at the process of face-to-face interaction with your child.

SHOULD YOU GIVE EXPLANATIONS?

The answer to this is a clear yes. And a clear no. It depends on what you mean by the term "explanation."

In my office I frequently watch parents attempt to explain their position to their children in a manner that sounds as if they are seeking the child's approval or agreement when there is something about their behavior that must change. I see mothers and fathers working too hard to explain themselves to a child who is resolutely refusing to understand. Mind you, it is usually not that the child is unable to understand. They are refusing to understand and hoping that the parents will cave in and back off.

Take the behavior that Brian displays. He's sixteen, a surfer type, and plenty bright. He's flunking all his classes and has a recent pattern of choosing druggies and drinkers for his friends. Whenever his mother talks to him, he looks away, rolls his eyes, and gives out a small sigh before answering. When I pointed this behavior out to him and indicated that it might have a great deal to do with the level of conflict he and his mother go through when they try to talk to each other, he told me he didn't understand why it would bother her. When I explained again in terms I believed to be clear enough for anyone capable of doing high school-level work, driving a car, and going to the beach by himself, he continued to insist that he could not understand what he was doing that would bug his mom so much. I decided to put it into terms he would understand. I asked him to assume he was at the beach and a beautiful girl came up and introduced herself. I asked him to assume that she looked at him and asked if he wanted to go make out. Then I asked him if he would be likely to look at her, roll his eyes, and sigh.

"No way," he said.

Despite the considerable difficulties, I advise explaining to children why you are placing limits on them, punishing them, or making certain demands on them. The purpose of an explanation is to provide your child with a chance to listen to reason and logic, hoping that reason and logic will convince them to modify their behavior. The intended goal is always that our children will listen, show some sort of insight, and give you a promise that they will attempt to change the negative behavior without your having to use coercive methods.

Sometimes simply sitting down and talking with oppositional children and teenagers works, but usually not. When oppositional children reject reason and logic, you must then plan to deliver an explanation that will be a mini-learning event that clearly sets out the consequences of choosing to ignore you. Such an event should be straightforward and brief.

Good explanations are statements of intent, not invitations to argue. Before giving an explanation to a child who has morphed into oppositional mode, sit with her alone and make it clear that you are about to tell her something that would be in her best interest to listen to. Let her know that if she fails to listen and make good decisions, then immediate consequences will follow.

THE COMPONENTS OF A GOOD EXPLANATION

A good explanation contains a number of components. You may want to listen to yourself talk the next time you have to place limits on your oppositional child to see how many of these components you use.

- A good explanation gives a child a chance to learn about the effect her behavior is having on you and on others and why the behavior must be modified as a result.

- It provides a clear explanation of the types of consequences she will encounter unless you see her working hard to modify her behavior.
- It provides a brief, clear description of replacement behaviors—ways of acting to replace her oppositional behaviors that will not lead to trouble for her but that will actually make her more successful.
- It contains replacement thoughts—ways of thinking to replace the mistaken, oppositional thinking that gets her into so much trouble.

Good explanations carry unspoken messages, usually implied by voice tone and posture. They indicate in a friendly but firm way, for example, that you are the parent and she is the child. Your role is not negotiable and you do not intend to abdicate your power. They make clear that you set the standards of behavior for members of your immediate family and that all behaviors have consequences. Positive behaviors on a child or teenager's part result in increased freedom and respect, while negative behaviors lead inexorably to punishment.

I encouraged Brian's mother to break out of the cycle of overexplaining, of being trapped in reason and logic. Like most parents, she found this to be a frustrating suggestion. Most adults make their living, in one way or another, by using reason and logic in situations in which a group consensus is necessary in order to proceed. If we try to use reason, logic, and consensus building when our children and teenagers are responding to us in an oppositional manner, the interaction is likely to degenerate into an argument.

I suggested to Brian's mother that she interact with him in a particular way, saying for instance: "I'm about to explain something to you that is very important for you to understand. I don't like it when you roll your eyes and sigh when I'm talking to you. It makes me angry, and if you continue to do it I will consider taking away your car keys for three days."

"I don't understand why it would bother you at all."

"It bothers me because I consider it to be rude. You would be smart to understand that most adults consider this type of behavior rude, and you would be smart to never expect me to accept it when you treat me in a rude manner. Before you answer me, make eye contact and please do not roll your eyes or sigh."

"I don't agree with that."

"I am not asking you to agree. What I am doing is telling you the effect your behavior has on me and letting you know that if you continue it, it will have a price."

"You can't tell me how to act."

"Your are perfectly right. I cannot make you or anyone else do anything. This is how I would like you to think: Your job is to decide how to act, and my job is to provide consequences. If you treat me well, you will continue to be able to use the car and the other things in our house. If you treat me badly, you will soon lose access to everything. I hope you make a smart decision."

We should stop the tape at this point and examine several things. The mother in this example is giving a number of messages in a relatively brief period. An interaction like this would take less than ninety seconds in real time. In this time she has let her son know that she is the parent and he is the child and that her role is not up for grabs. She has implied to him that he is not equal to her in the family power structure and that she sets the standards for his behavior. She has given him a clear replacement behavior to use instead of his negative behavior and has indicated to him how he might think about their interactions. She has made clear that his negative behaviors will have a guaranteed cost and that he can avoid the cost by making a smart decision. Not once did she appear to ask his permission or to be overly concerned about whether or not he agreed with her parental demands. And, she didn't spend half an evening arguing.

ISOLATE THEM TO AVOID PEER REINFORCEMENT AND EMBARRASSMENT

One thing many oppositional children and teenagers love is demonstrating in front of their peers or siblings that you cannot make them do anything. For example, in the classroom when the teacher has asked someone to be silent, he might respond, "You can't make me!" Or if you tell your kid to leave the room because she's arguing with everyone, she might mutter on the way out, "You're stupid." Times like this are when all eyes are on them. These are the moments they live for.

The best thing to do at moments like these, whether in the classroom or the home, is to remove the child to another room to talk. This shuts off the social reinforcement of having her friends, brothers, or sisters watch her bravely take you on. In the home, if she refuses to leave the room with you, have the other children leave. This is imperative, because when she has an audience she will not listen or deal with you in a straightforward manner. When she has an audience all she will do is perform.

There is another reason to remove the child from the room—to avoid embarrassing her in front of her peers or siblings. If you are like many parents, your reasoning might be that laying on a bit of shame or guilt in front of the other kids might teach her a lesson. In reality it is more likely to solidify her viewpoint that the adult is the enemy.

A deeper reason yet exists for avoiding shame and guilt. Just because a child or teenager is oppositional and defiant does not mean that she does not have interior, private thoughts about herself. Once she is an adult, given that her thoughts and beliefs control her behavior much like a computer program controls a computer, she will act in the world based on her beliefs about herself and others. For prepubescent children in particular that computer program is constantly being modified by external input. If you repeatedly shame a child by punishing her in front of her friends or by telling her she is dumb or stupid or bad, the results extend far beyond your moment of anger. It becomes part of what she believes about herself. At the cost of repeating myself, this is how it works: She comes to hate herself. Anyone who hates herself becomes angry. She acts her anger out on the world. She raises a child who hates herself, and so on.

There is a logic to an oppositional child's internal world. They act oppositionally, talk oppositionally, and think oppositionally as their first line of defense in a world they view as hostile toward them. This is easy to observe. Go to a convenience store near a high school around lunch time during the school year. In many ways it is humorous to see the skinny ninth grade boys spitting and standing with their hips thrust out, smoking and looking contrary. The convenience store parking lot at lunch time often looks like a developmental kindergarten for bad guys.

Given the defensiveness of these children and teens, it is important that you do not expect them to easily open up when you isolate them to talk. Defensive people, whether children or adults, usually do not have a strong conscious grasp on what they think and feel about themselves. Your job as the parent is to understand how they see the world and why they act the way they do, even when they don't understand it.

A final point about this is that they often do not expect adults to act like they like them. By being alone with them and acting in a firm but friendly manner even when they are defensive, you open the door a crack to helping them see that they can be alone with others and be engaged in a conversation instead of an argument.

GIVE CLEAR MESSAGES ABOUT NEGATIVE BEHAVIORS AND THEIR COSTS

All behaviors have costs associated with them. If you try to be the class clown, but your joke falls flat, your cost is embarrassment in front of your peers. Oppositional children, being optimistic, fail to take into account that their oppositional behavior might have a cost associated with it. All they see is the potential reward.

From a reinforcement perspective, it is good for negative behaviors to cost more than they are worth. Many infants go through a period when they bite other people's ankles. Although some parents view this as a time to use spanking, I've found that using a kitchen baster (the type with a squeeze bulb) to blow a puff of air into the child's face is just as effective as a deterrent. They don't like getting the puff of air in the face, and if you deliver the puff of air every time they bite you, they soon change their behavior.

I wish I could tell you that blowing into your oppositional teenager's face will cause him to change his behavior. No such luck, I'm afraid. Instead, you have to make it perfectly clear to him what his negative behaviors will cost, and you have to find a way to prove to him that you will provide consequences over and over and over and over. Remember, he is oppositional and believes that he can outlast you.

I ask parents to sit down with their kids and go over a list of behaviors that will always result in punishment. They will often try to be tricky about your list, so be clear that you expect them to use good reasoning. Otherwise you will find them saying things to you like, "But you never told me I had to turn in my homework. You only said I had to do it."

As you progress through the list, make sure you connect a cost to each behavior. For example, "When you insult me, like telling me I'm stupid, my first response will be to have you go to your room and think about what you did for about half an hour. You shouldn't expect to watch any TV for the rest of the evening, and you won't be allowed to leave the house. You'll also lose your video game privileges for the evening."

ASK MORAL QUESTIONS

You won't know how your child thinks unless you ask the right questions. Unless your child reveals his thoughts to you, you will have little opportunity to help him correct the mistaken thoughts that lead to his oppositional behavior.

For example, one of the questions many mental health professionals use when trying to find out how a person is likely to think and behave is to ask them what they would do if they were to lose something that belongs to a friend. Most non-oppositional children will give answers like "Buy them another one," "Give them one of mine," or "Give them money so they can buy a new one." Oppositional children, juvenile delinquents in particular, answer by saying, "Tell them." There is no implication of personal responsibility to correct the mistake. They will sometimes say, "There's nothing you can do, it's lost," or even just shrug their shoulders.

This is one of those places where you have to give yourself room to be creative. You can ask your child questions like the one above, but there are lots of other things to ask that might reveal how your child's mind really works. What would you do if you found a wallet full of money on the sidewalk and it had the owners name and phone number in it? How should you respond to your teacher when she tells you to sit down and you know your friends are watching? What do you do when your parents say be home by ten but your friends tell you that letting your parents boss you around is for chumps?

In general, if your child acts oppositionally but can give you reasonable answers to your questions and has a tendency to moderate his or her behavior at school or at a friend's house, half the battle is already won. This tells you he knows right from wrong but is having difficulty implementing it at home, which is a common pattern. The child who draws a blank when you ask him moral questions or who is oppositional to most people in most settings is the one I really worry about. Should this be your child, your task is to teach him how most other people think and to help him see that people who stay out of trouble not only act differently from him, but also think differently. You want to help him understand that it is the thinking differently that causes the acting differently.

Ask your preadolescent child to think of two other kids he goes to school with, one who stays in trouble and one who hardly ever gets into trouble. Ask him how he thinks each of these two would respond to the question about finding the wallet or losing something that belongs to a friend. Ask if he can see how one way of thinking keeps one kid in trouble and how the other way of thinking keeps the other kid out of trouble. Then ask him to compare his own thinking to the two example children. Ask which of his thoughts he needs to replace with thoughts that will keep him out of trouble, and be sure to give him examples if he has trouble. After all, this level of self-confrontation can be difficult for a child. Talk daily to your child about replacing the thoughts that lead him into trouble with thoughts that will help him stay out of trouble.

I also play a game with young oppositional children in which I ask them to pretend that I have a speaker in my brain that will allow them to hear my thoughts. I ask them to help me find out which of my thoughts will help me stay out of trouble and which of my thoughts will be likely to get me in trouble. Once they learn to identify my "trouble" thoughts, I ask them to help me replace these thoughts with "no trouble" thoughts. I reward them with praise, rounds of applause, and high fives when they begin to come up with "no trouble" thoughts for me to think and for them to copy in their own lives.

AVOID SPRAYING MATCHES WITH SKUNKS

A number of years ago I served as an intern on a chronic pain unit. The patients there had been hurt in industrial accidents, falls, car wrecks, and so on. They had lots of reasons to be cranky and disagreeable. But one patient there was the absolute king of opposition. He was an attorney and was highly successful. Maybe part of what made him so good was that he was exceptionally defensive. He had a rationalization for everything—to the point that it was impossible to get him to acknowledge that he had made any mistakes or misjudgments. The other patients had come to me in secret to complain about the blunt, hurtful comments he would make about them during group sessions and how he dominated the group's talk time with his victory stories. I found him to be irritating, and I have to admit that I thought he needed to be brought down a peg or two.

I decided during our group session to confront him about his effect on others. Keep in mind that he was a seasoned trial lawyer and I was an earnest young psychologist who believed in the power of psychological interpretation to help people become less defensive. He ate me for lunch.

My supervising psychologist, a wizened veteran himself, pulled me aside and gave me some of the best advice I've ever received. "Don't get in a spraying match with a skunk," he said.

Oppositional children and teenagers are like this attorney. I jokingly refer to them as skunks. They are better than anyone else at being oppositional, and if you attempt to teach them a lesson by being oppositional and aggressive yourself, you won't win. For you to act oppositionally is (hopefully) artificial. For them, it is as natural as their name. You cannot beat oppositional children at their own game. This is why they try to draw you into arguments—they know that you do not have the ability to make them admit they have done anything wrong. Oppositional and defiant children know when someone is playing a game with them because they are skilled at reading the nuances of human behavior. Don't be confused by the fact that they sometimes lack the verbal skills to explain what they know or to do well in the classroom. They know a lot about human motivation and manipulation.

You Can't Talk to a Drunk When He's Drinking

Lengthy, serious discussions about a person's negative behavior cannot be done in the midst of that behavior. Trying to have a conversation with an oppositional child or teenager about her behavior during an oppositional outburst is like trying to talk to a drunken alcoholic about her drinking. If you have ever been unfortunate enough to have done the latter, you know why it will not work for the former.

It is best to find a time to talk to your child or teenager when you can be alone with her, when she is in a good mood, and when the tension in the home is low. Explain to her that you are going to talk to her about oppositional behavior. Give her a clear explanation about what oppositional behavior is. Most children and teenagers respond best when you talk to them about someone else's oppositional behavior—someone they know, someone you know currently, or someone you knew when you were your child's age. In particular, they like it if you tell them stories about your own oppositional behaviors when you were their age. Your child will be aware the conversation will get around to her. Starting by discussing others will make her less defensive, make her realize that she is not the only person with this particular problem, and give her a chance to laugh about what oppositional children and teens really look like when she stands back and observes them.

Help Them to Recognize Their Oppositional Behavior

As you review how oppositional children think, ask your child or teen if he thinks that way too. Younger kids are prone to admit that they do, maybe even wondering if you can read their minds by knowing that they have such thoughts. The teenagers are prone to deny ever thinking that way, but they will admit that plenty of their friends do.

Once you establish with him that he uses oppositional thinking at times, your next step is to ask him how often acting oppositional gets him in trouble. Usually oppositional children will admit that their defiant ways cause them trouble. Ask your child if he stays in trouble more than most people his age. This may be another one of those tricky junctures. For one thing, if most of his friends are oppositional (and they do all tend to seek out others with similar attitudes), then he is likely to tell you no, he's not in any more trouble than his friends, thank you very much. He's also likely to use this point as proof that you are wrong and he is right. Instead, you have to get him to compare himself to someone else you both know who is not an oppositional type but who is also acceptable to him. Otherwise, he is likely to tell you that you are asking him to compare himself to nerds and geeks, and he would rather be in trouble than be one of those. Once you find the acceptable point of comparison, oppositional kids typically will admit that they get in more trouble than a lot of others their age.

Offer Replacement Behaviors, Replacement Thoughts

Praise your child for being honest and insightful if you get to this point with him. It is at this point that you should try an extended discussion about replacement behaviors and replacement thoughts.

Again, take it slow. Take advantage of the opportunity, but don't try to get it all solved in one talk.

The replacement behaviors and thoughts are not as hard to come up with as you might imagine. Review the types of behaviors and beliefs that we discussed in chapter 1, and simply state their opposites. Here is an example, using the technique of talking about someone else to make the subject more palatable: "I bet you know lots of people who always try to prove that the adults are wrong. I knew lots of people who were that way when I was fifteen. The problem was, they were always in trouble and always getting punished. Most of the guys I knew stayed in trouble until they decided it was better to try to get along with people instead of always trying to prove them wrong."

In a moment we'll discuss a list of replacements. But first, it is important that you give your child or teen a way and a reason to accept the replacements. She will resist the idea that she has to change because it might mean conceding failure. I tell oppositional teenagers that they need to learn to be "bilingual" because it will increase their chances of getting what they want. I suggest that it is okay to use all of the oppositional attitude they want when they are hanging out with their friends. They just need to turn it off once they encounter adults or other people they don't know. With the younger ones I point out that by changing their oppositional behaviors, they are much less likely to be in trouble with teachers and parents.

Here are a list of replacement thoughts and behaviors you might want to discuss with your oppositional child or teenager:

- It's really not possible to defeat all the adults. They own everything and will take it away if you make them too mad.
- It's good to be optimistic. But use your optimism to plan how to win a game or a contest, not to plan how to always prove people wrong.

- If you fail to learn from experience, you'll repeat the same mistake over and over. That means getting punished for the same thing time and time again.
- Don't expect others to treat you fairly unless you treat them fairly. You are not the sole judge of whether or not you treated them fairly. You may say you did, but they may say you didn't. Both opinions must be considered.
- Revenge is not always the best option. There are thousands of people who believe you should get revenge on whoever makes you mad. Visit a prison any time to ask the inmates how well their strategies worked.
- It's a mistake to believe that nice people are weak. Go pose that question to a local karate instructor.
- When you use the tiniest flaw in what someone is saying to try to prove that they are totally wrong, you only leave an impression of yourself as being unwilling to consider opinions other than your own.
- Few people believe that children and teens are equal to adults. They share an equal right not to be harmed, but otherwise children have yet to accumulate enough experience to be treated as anything but their age.
- People who remain ignorant of their impact on others are doomed to live in a world in which they believe others punish them because they're jealous of them, or because they don't like them due to a personal characteristic such as race, sex, or religion. Although this does occur, the most frequent reason for disliking someone is their behavior.
- Any adult who acts hostile or unfriendly toward you for no reason at all has a problem, and it is best to stay away from him. However, no one is likely to believe that almost every adult you encounter acts hostile or unfriendly toward you for no reason at all.

- If you answer questions with "I don't know," pretty soon people will come to believe that you are stupid. It is much better to say "Give me a second to think about it," or "I don't know right now, but I'll try to find out more and let you know later." Afterward, you have to follow up.
- If you believe that parents will run out of moves if you ignore their attempts to use reason and logic, you're wrong. By ignoring reason and logic, you invite parents to use drastic solutions.

ADMIRE THEIR ATTEMPTS TO BE STRONG

Attempts to talk to oppositional children and teenagers are doomed to fail if they are limited only to laying down the law and setting limits. Oppositional children and teenagers view themselves as fighting for their rights. The main mistake they make is to assume that you are trying to contravene their rights by setting limits on them. You must let them know that you admire their attempts to be strong and to stand up for themselves. Tell them it is only the form that their attempts take that you disagree with, because they tend to create trouble with others.

Keep in mind that these are not children who are used to being admired. They are used to being disagreed with and being punished. Being admired is something that does not come to them often enough, from their perspective. They tend to forget that you can still like them even though you are in the midst of a conflict with them. Your attempt to insert this fact into your interaction with them may have a soothing effect on the part of them that is filled with anger.

When your child is in the midst of an oppositional outburst, try complimenting them on their strength, their ability to argue, or on their integrity. This will almost always catch them off guard. It usually helps to calm the situation, assuming you use the technique early enough in the argument and assuming you can convey that you are genuine in what you are saying.

This once worked with a seventeen-year-old boy I knew. He was bright, intense, but humorless, with a long history of running away, staying out late with inappropriate friends, and general defiance of family rules. His general argument to me was that at his age he should be allowed to make his own rules and that he did not understand why he did not have the same amount of power in his family that the adults had. I explained to him as clearly as I could that I knew of no high-functioning family that gave teenagers decision-making power equal to the adults. I explained that high-functioning families certainly listen closely to their teenagers and accord them vast amounts of freedom if trust has been earned and maintained (which for him was not the case). I told him that in all family structures I was aware of there was a hierarchy, with adults at the top and everyone else below them.

This put him into a long, impassioned speech on how this was not fair and just because it had always been done this way does not mean it works, and just because it might work for other families does not mean it would work for his family, and so on.

At the end of our session I took the time to compliment him on his use of reason and logic and his ability to hold his position in an argument. I indicated to him that I did not agree with his conclusions, but that I could see his considerable intellect coming through in his words, and I found much to admire about him. As he left, he smiled at me. When he came back for our second meeting he was much less argumentative and willing to begin to examine which of his actions and behaviors created the most trouble for him with his parents.

I am certain that there are many other successful strategies for talking with oppositional children and teenagers. You should feel free to integrate them into your own methods. Be sure to remember that oppositional arguing by children or teens really is an attempt to communicate, regardless of the fact that it is a failed attempt. Remember that what they are trying to communicate is their frustration over their lack of power or influence. Don't get pulled off into secondary issues. Instead, talk to them about how to get the power and influence that is available to them at their age if they are more careful about their behaviors and beliefs. Finally, remember that at times even such fair-minded talk will fail. We will examine next what to do when this happens.

CHAPTER FIVE

When Talk Fails

Sooner or later attempts to use talk as a method of intervention with an oppositional child or teenager will fail. At times, he will simply do what he wants, regardless of what you say. Some of this is common and healthy in children and teenagers. As an everyday lifestyle, though, it leaves much to be desired.

As indicated earlier, oppositional kids often believe that, if they ignore you long enough, you will eventually give up. Instead of falling into this trap, as many parents do, you need to move on to the next level of intervention. You will find that, instead of there being nothing to do, there are literally hundreds of things you can do. The first task is to find a place to start.

In the grand scheme of psychological interventions, talk is always the desired place to start. It teaches children the value of using reason and being logical, the value of cooperative decision making, and the ability to listen to feedback on their behavior. Oppositional children are often psychologically brittle, though. Although they look vigorous and brave, they have little ability to take feedback about themselves from others. They lash out or dig their heels in rather than admit they have done anything wrong. From their perspective, if you tell them they have done something bad, it is like telling them they are no good at all. This is why they fight so vigorously to dis-prove what you are saying.

In some families when talk fails, the emotional equivalent of nuclear holocaust begins. The parents overrespond or overreact, and their attempts to solve the problem of oppositionality become as illogical and irrational as the child's behavior itself. Although it is not good to underrespond to an oppositional child, neither is it good to overrespond.

It is better to have a sense of what your number-two strategy should be when talk fails, and, should number two fail, what to use for number three, number four, and so on. Each new level of response should be a little more intense than the one preceding it. Fifteen minutes of time out in your kid's room is not nearly as intense as losing access to phone, bike, and friends all day, for example.

The list of possible responses is best thought of as a hierarchy. You proceed from responses that limit your child in only minor ways all the way up to the level where most of her freedoms are suspended. Somewhere along the way you will manage to get her attention.

When talk fails, the next step is to move to a clear warning about what your child's behavior is about to cost her. If warnings fail, and they will until you teach your child that it is best to heed them, you must move into an action-oriented strategy, one in which the move-ment and privileges of the oppositional child are suspended. If your initial withdrawal of privileges is not successful, you begin to remove more and for longer periods. We will go through all of the proce-dures in more detail below. At this point we'll return to the idea of warning systems. When used properly, they often give your child just enough feedback to get her to stop whatever oppositional behavior she is engaged in. Remember, don't use punishment if a warning will work.

WARNING SYSTEMS

The first type of warning, as we've already seen, is the verbal warning. It should indicate to your child what the offending behavior is, what the costs may be, and what the replacement behaviors and thoughts might be. Some children do not respond to verbal warnings. If you find that verbal warnings do not work for your child, you should feel free to try different types of warning systems. In general, the procedures below are for prepubescent children and will not work well with jaded, worldly teenager types. For teenagers, verbal warnings are the only realistic strategies to employ. They must learn that if they do not heed the verbal warning, you will move forward with punishment without arguing and explaining yourself.

Many parents find that one sort of warning system will work for a number of weeks or months, but then it loses its impact. This is common with many systems of behavior feedback when they are used in the home over long periods, and it is nothing to worry about. When it happens, simply move to another system or use a combination of two or more systems. Experiment to find what works best for your family and be willing to make modifications as necessary. A particularly important tip is to not get discouraged too quickly. When you bring a new form of psychological intervention into the life of an oppositional child, her first move will be to ignore it. Her second will be to attempt to defeat it. It is not uncommon for parents to return to my office after a week of trying a particular procedure with their child and say to me, "It doesn't work." In most cases I ask them to try it for a month before they decide it doesn't work. Be aware that if your child continues to believe that she can defeat you, no system of warning will work. Warning systems work only when you have given your child a clear message that her oppositional behavior will lead to real consequences. A variety of warning procedures follow. Before employing one of them, sit down with your child and explain it clearly to her, and let her know you will be using it.

One-Two-Three System

There are a number of variations of this age-old procedure, which is also called Three Strikes. Tell your child that when you find him acting in a manner that is unacceptable, you will ask him to make eye contact with you, and then you will say "one."

Let him know that you will be willing to give him a brief description of his offending behavior. You should not be willing to argue or go into detail. Then explain to him that should the behavior persist, after a few minutes you say "two." If he fails to cease the offending behavior, after a few minutes you will say "three." Once you reach three, he is "out," and a period of punishment begins. The particular procedures and suggestions for punishments will follow in a later section.

The beauty of this system is that it gives parents an easy way to avoid argument. Your response to unacceptable behavior is one word, but it delivers a strong message. If you say "one," the child is placed on warning. It's like telling him to play it smart, worse things might be coming. If you are forced to say "two," you give him notice that he has been given all of the warnings he is going to get. "Three" is self-explanatory.

With such a system, the parent should feel free to deliver the first warning of at 10:00 in the morning, for example, and go to the second at noon if the child has been good but negative behavior is beginning to return. The parent can also return to "one" for the next warning if significant time has passed and the child has been behaving well. The ground rule is that you don't want to move all the way to "three" too quickly. Neither, however, do you want to drone on with "one" or "two" all day and never let your child experience the consequences of his behavior. As with most systems, you will have to try it out to find how rapidly to pace your movement from one to two to three. Your pacing may much depend upon how willing or unwilling your child is to heed your warnings.

Yellow Card System

I adapted this for my own use after my children got involved in soccer. In soccer, the referee shows a player a yellow card once she has committed an offense and tells her what the offense was. Then play resumes. The yellow card is a warning. You can get two such warnings in a game. After the next offense, you get shown a red card and you are out of the game.

This system works well for families who like sports and who value humor. You can cut two three-by-five squares of heavy construction paper and color one yellow and one red. Let your child know that you will show her a yellow card after your initial verbal warning has failed. If she persists, after a brief period you will show her the yellow card again. If she still fails to stop the negative behavior, you will show her the red card, which indicates to her that she is out of the game and will be punished.

Red-Yellow-Green Stoplight System

This system is similar to those above in that it also uses a system of three signals. It is different, however, in that it is a more continuous form of feedback. In order to use it, take a sheet of paper, fold it into thirds, and tape the ends together. Stand it on end and you will have a triangle-shaped tower. Color one side red, one side yellow, and one side green.

In this system you place the tower where it can be seen. The top of your refrigerator might work, as would a counter top. If the green side of the tower is facing outward, that is a sign to your child that his behavior is appropriate and that he is safe to proceed. Should his behavior turn oppositional and negative, you turn the yellow face of the tower to the room and tell your child to go check the signal. The yellow signal, as with a stoplight, indicates to him that he should proceed with caution. Should his negative behavior persist, you may turn the signal so that the red side is facing outward, which means that he will receive punishment.

Doomsday Clock

This is borrowed from the doomsday-countdown clock of the Union of Concerned Scientists, the clock that measures how far away the world is from a nuclear war. Use cardboard to make a round clock face that has only the numbers nine, ten, eleven, and twelve. The clock needs only one hand. When the hand of the clock points to nine, that tells the child that he is not in jeopardy of punishment and that he is doing fine. When his behavior begins to become unacceptable, move the clock hand to ten and bring it to his attention. Should he not change his behavior, move the hand to eleven and again insist that he go look at the clock. Once the hand moves to twelve, he will receive punishment. If his behavior has improved after the hand has been moved to ten or eleven, you can move the hand back down. If, for example, the hand was set at eleven and your child made a strong effort to control his behavior over the next hour, you should feel free to move the hand back to nine. If his behavior was marginally improved and you believed that it would provide a positive incentive to continue trying, you could move the hand back to ten.

Check/Self-Check

I devised this primarily to use with prepubescent children who display high frequencies of negative behaviors. For kids in kindergarten to second grade, this might mean being stubborn and oppositional in addition to hitting or pushing other kids, taking things away from them, or disrupting working groups. For older children—third grade through fifth grade—it is useful for those who often engage in negative behaviors such as arguing, demanding, fighting, bothering others, and so on and who are so caught up in what they are doing that their ability to stop themselves is marginal. Check/Self-Check is used to make them aware of what they are doing so that they do not allow themselves simply to be on automatic pilot, a habit common to oppositional children. It also works well for hyperactive children, many of whom are oppositional in nature.

The best way to teach Check/Self-Check to your child is to role-play. You pretend to be the child, and your child pretends to be the parent. Tell your child to instruct you that it is time to do one of your chores. Let her know that after she does, you will respond in a highly oppositional, defiant manner. Tell her that when you begin to act this way she should look at you and say in a firm voice, "Check." Explain that when she gives you the command to check yourself, you will pretend that the "speaker in your brain" is turned on so that she will be able to hear you think about what you need to do to check yourself. The role-playing exchange might go like this:

Child (as parent): "Jill, it's time to feed the cats."

Parent (as child), talking in an angry tone, balling her fists, and thrashing around in her chair: "I'm tired of feeding those stupid cats! I hate having to feed them. Why can't I get some fish instead?"

"Jill, check yourself."

Parent can then go into what looks like slow motion and appear to think out loud: "Let's see now, I was just yelling at my mom, so I better control my voice. I had my fists all balled up, so I'm going to relax my hands. I had an angry look on my face, so I better change that. I'm going to sit up in my chair and not bounce around." Parent then sits up, makes eye contact, and says, "OK mom, I'm checked."

Let's go through this, piece by piece. It is much easier for a child to learn what the command "check" means if you act it out for her. Trying to explain it does not work well at all. When you act out the process of checking yourself, you let your child see that you are analyzing not only what you are saying but also your voice tone, facial expression, and movement. In brief, you give yourself critical feedback on what you said, how you said it, and how you could correct it.

After you act it out, switch roles and do it again. Let your child be the child, and you be the adult. When you tell her to check, have her pretend that she has turned on the speaker in her brain so that you can hear what she is thinking. I should add that some children have trouble articulating the behaviors that need correcting. As long as they are able to correct themselves, however, your goal is at least partially met. Be sure to let them know that once you begin to use the "check" command at home, they are not expected to turn on their "speaker" anyway. Again, the main goal is that your child knows how to rapidly correct her behavior when it veers into unacceptable territory.

Once your child is up to speed on this procedure, use it when she is beginning to act in an oppositional manner. Make eye contact, say her name in a friendly but firm manner, and say "check." If you or your child do not like the term "check," invent your own term. The main point is to have a verbal warning to let her know she needs to make a quick change in what she is doing.

The second aspect of this procedure is the self-check. You should explain to your child that as she learns more about her own behavior, you hope she will do a self-check. That is, you hope she'll begin to catch herself when she's behaving defiantly and correct herself without prompting. Once you decide she is ready to monitor herself, role-play with her again. This time, you are again the child and your behavior is turning oppositional. Let her observe the thought process involved in a self-check by turning on the speaker again.

Parent: "Jill, it's your turn to take out the trash."

Child: "Don't bother me right now, can't you see I'm in the middle of my video game. Get Ben to take out the trash, he never . . ." Child pauses for a second and begins to think out loud. "I was yelling at my mom again, and I had a mean look on my face. I wasn't looking at her when she was talking to me." Child catches herself, sits upright, ceases thrashing about and frowning, and makes eye contact. "Mom, I just did a self-check."

Switch roles and let your child practice doing a self-check. Some children will be proud of their ability to do this, at least at first. It is important that you praise them for effective self-checks. They will begin to see that it is a special ability that will make them more successful.

Some children will complain vociferously that it is stupid to use these methods, particularly if they are close to puberty. Other children will like them because they provide a clear type of feedback. For children who do not like these methods or who say they are dumb or stupid, indicate that it is indeed rather silly to have to resort to these techniques when they are perfectly capable of responding to your verbal warnings and of learning to monitor their behavior on their own. Make it clear that once they are able to respond quickly to your verbal warnings, you will not have to use these sorts of tools.

For children who like these methods, make sure they get involved with how and when to use them. Some children like designing the clock, the red-yellow-green tower, or the soccer cards. If they welcome the feedback, allow them to make suggestions for what kinds of behaviors will result in a warning and what kinds of behaviors will result in praise. Some younger children will suggest that you be harder on them than you would actually need to be. Take this as a sign of the desire to correct their behavior, and make sure the behaviors you punish truly violate age-appropriate norms in an unacceptable manner.

WHEN WARNINGS FAIL: ACTION-ORIENTED INTERVENTIONS

Just as talk will often fail with oppositional children and teens, so will warnings. Remember, their strategy is to ignore you because they believe that you will either give up or run out of options. When warnings fail, the next step is an action-oriented intervention. It's time to put your money where your mouth is.

I suggest that your first action-oriented intervention is time out. As I discussed earlier in this section, the interventions need to start at a relatively mild level and move forward in intensity until you have the child or teenager's attention. If a mild intervention gets their attention, fine. If it takes devoting every spare minute of your time and using intensive interventions, then you must be prepared to do so. The most basic intervention involves having your child sit quietly in his room, or another spot, to reflect upon what needs to change about his behavior. No privileges are lost in the most basic type of time out. The most intense interventions involve high levels of restriction and complete loss of access to reinforcers. I'll discuss each of these levels separately.

Time Out

Time out is best conceptualized as a period a child must spend thinking about how his thoughts and behaviors have gotten him into trouble and how to replace those thoughts and behaviors with others that will not cause trouble. Time out is not itself a punishment, at least at the early stages of intervention. It should be used by your child to sit and think about how to make better decisions and about how to use the replacement behaviors and replacement thoughts you have previously urged him to use. Time out should always begin with a brief, clear description of the behaviors that have gotten the child in trouble along with an explanation of how long the time out will be. It should end with a brief discussion of the decisions your child has come to about new behaviors, new thoughts, and how to stay out of trouble.

Time out generally will not work with children who are below the age of three and a half. Very young children often fail to understand its purpose. With these children it is best to explain what they have done wrong and then role-play with them to show them how it could have been done better. You might also consider strategies like removing them from the room where they are acting in an unacceptable way and redirecting them to a new activity. They will rarely be able to sit in their rooms or in chairs for time out.

Time out with children between the ages of four and six generally takes place in their rooms and is relatively brief. A four-year-old might be given eight to ten minutes to sit and think about how she got herself in trouble and how not to do it again soon (at least within the next half hour). Some five-year-olds might be given ten minutes of time-out, and six-year-olds can be given up to fifteen minutes.

For children ages seven, eight, and nine, time out should not exceed twenty minutes. In general, this also holds true for ten-, eleven-, and twelve-year-olds. I do not recommend using time out for children over the age of twelve and will discuss this below.

What I've just described is basic time out, the type you use after warnings have failed. When the basic time out fails to help your child change his behavior, it is time to reconsider whether the intensity of the time out is sufficient. Before you consider lengthening the time out, ask yourself how your child is spending the time-out period. Is he actually thinking of new ways to act and think or is he drawing, reading books, or taking a nap? Far too often a parent simply sends the child to his room, waits twenty minutes, and then shouts up to him that he can come out. Maybe he was using the time productively. But if his behavior remains oppositional, chances are he used the time-out period to check out his baseball card collection, or listen to the latest CD on his headphones. Don't automatically assume that time away from you feels like punishment to children.

If your child is not using time out in a productive way, give him explicit instructions on how to use it. Again, tell him that he is to think about how his behavior and thinking got him into trouble and about how he might replace the faulty behaviors and thoughts. More importantly at this point, he should receive instructions that during time out in his room he is not to sleep, listen to music, read magazines, draw, or do anything else other than think about what you have told him to think about. Only after you have made it this explicit should you consider upping the intensity of the time out.

Intensity of Time Out

The main way to increase the intensity of time out is to increase the time the child has to stay in his room. This does not work with children under the age of about four, however, and I recommend this tactic be reserved for children between ages six and twelve. To make time out more punishing, simply double it. For example, if you normally give your child about twenty minutes in his room to think, but it doesn't seem to do any good, then consider giving him up to forty. Older children, closer to age twelve, can be given up to one hour, but there's little point in extending it further. Chances are, if they haven't used the time to think after being in their room for one hour, they aren't going to use time out to think at all. You will be forced to move to yet another level of intensity.

There is one serious exception to these time limits. If you tell your child that she has to go into her room for a twenty-minute time out and she spends the twenty minutes slamming doors, throwing things, yelling at you to let her out, or crying hysterically enough to alarm the neighbors, from my perspective, she has not completed time out. Parents should inform their child that the time out clock starts running only when she is in control of herself. If she yells, kicks, and screams, and it takes her several hours to do a twenty-minute time out, then she learns a valuable lesson about the fact that you mean what you say. If you give in, then you train her to believe that she can defeat you by yelling, kicking, and screaming. It is important to remember here the necessary ideas for parenting an oppositional child, especially that you must be willing to allow your child to be unhappy in such situations.

Combining Time Out with Loss of Reinforcers

Let's assume that you have now tried the forms of time out we've talked about above, and your child continues to remain oppositional. This is a signal to you that it is time to use as much time out as is advisable, plus add the new dimension of loss of access to reinforcers.

This will require a look at what comprises reinforcers for the typical child and teenager, and after this we will return to how to use time out and loss of access to reinforcers in combination.

ACCESS TO REINFORCERS AND PRIVILEGES

Reinforcers are the good things in life that we all seek, an activity or object that has inherent worth to us. I also use the word "privilege" because when we use it in the traditional middle-class sense it has the implication that something has been earned. In most middle-class homes having a bicycle and time to ride it is earned through good behavior and is not an inalienable right granted by higher powers.

Privileges and reinforcers come in many forms. They may be favored foods or drinks, activities, use of objects and devices, favored clothes items, and so on. The list is potentially endless, and each person's list is highly individual. While my main reinforcers might be things like going to play tennis, going to movies, or listening to music, yours might be going to dinner, wearing your favorite shoes, and painting, drawing, or fishing.

In order for you to get control of an oppositional child or teenager, you must be willing to take control of their reinforcers and make sure that they do not have access to them unless earned by appropriate behavior. You do not want to deviate from the rule that reinforcers are earned, because doing so teaches children that they have the right to have fun and to use their goodies regardless of their behavior.

As we discussed previously, there are two levels of reinforcers, the obvious and the subtle. The obvious reinforcers include things such as television, bicycles, video games, stereos and headphones, cars, computers, friends, telephones, money, and so on. Subtle reinforcers include things many parents never consider withholding from their children, such as access to their cool tennis shoes and T-shirts (the kind with sports team or rock band logos); snacks, treats, or desserts; long showers or baths; magazines, newspapers, or books; make-up and jewelry; or paper and pencil for drawing.

You will also recall that we discussed the idea that everything in the home belongs to the parents. This extends to all the reinforcers, both obvious and subtle.

I suggest to parents that when they are in situations where a child or teen's behavior has become extreme, they must be willing to prove to the child that he does not in fact legally own anything. If it is necessary to remove things that the child or teenager has purchased with his own money or things that have been given to him, parents must be willing to do so. You must do whatever it takes to get his attention and to get him to comply with the family's rules and standards.

In general, a child or teen's access to reinforcers should be in inverse proportion to her oppositional behavior. The more oppositional she is, the fewer reinforcers she should have access to. It follows that the longer she stays negative, the longer she loses access. When she begins to improve, her reinforcers come back.

When it comes to limiting reinforcers, the general practice is to remove access to several of the most important ones for periods ranging from an hour to three hours, depending on circumstances. In many cases when your ten-year-old has slapped you with a load of oppositional attitude, it will suffice to give him an hour in his room to think about the bad decision he made and to remove access to his bike, headphones, and skateboard for the afternoon.

For some children this is enough. However, you must be prepared for the oppositional child who will not get the point until he has lost access to absolutely everything.

Let me make this perfectly clear: You must be willing to take away their access to *everything*. Depending on how well or how poorly they respond, you must be willing to take away their access to everything for periods ranging from several hours to days—whatever is necessary to get them to change their oppositional behavior.

A conversation with an oppositional female teenager who is about to experience loss of all obvious and subtle reinforcers might go something like this:

Parent: "I've given you a number of warnings about talking back to me, and you seem to have ignored them. I have also suggested alternative ways you might act toward me and alternative ways to think about your role in our family that might keep you out of trouble. Since you have ignored me, I'm now removing everything for the rest of the afternoon."

Teen: "What do you mean by everything?"

Parent: "It means you will not be allowed to leave the house for the next four hours. During that time you won't go outside, have phone calls, watch TV, listen to your headphones, go to your room, take a nap, take a bath or shower, have snacks or anything to drink, or do anything else that you would normally want to do. You won't be allowed to do anything but think about how to change your behavior."

Teen: "You can't make me do that."

Parent: "You're quite right. I can't make anyone do anything. I will tell you, though, that if you refuse to do this on your own, I will take away all of your privileges for even longer. You would be smart to go along with this."

Teen: "What if I don't?"

Parent: "There is no rule that tells me I can't take away everything you use here at home for as long as I please. I only have to provide you with a roof over your head, a few clothes, and enough food to keep you healthy. Everything else is optional. You need to understand that I am willing to take away everything until I am satisfied with your behavior."

Teen: "What if I just leave?"

Parent: "I'll do everything possible to find you. When I find you, or when you come home, instead of losing everything for the afternoon, you'll lose it for much longer."

Teen: "How long?"

Parent: "Until I'm satisfied with you behavior. If it takes a month, that will be your decision."

It's probably about this time that the oppositional teenager stomps off, and if she is smart, she begins to grudgingly comply.

Monster Time Out

There is a variation of this strategy of taking away all obvious and subtle reinforcers that I use with prepubescent children, those typically between ages six and twelve. I call it Monster Time Out. I joke with parents that the "monster" part of this term refers to the intensity of the time out, not to the child. These are the ground rules: In Monster Time Out a child can't do anything for four hours. He can't watch TV or listen to music. If he is in a room where there is a TV or stereo and someone else wants to watch or listen, he must leave the room. He can't go into his bedroom to lie down, take a nap or do anything fun. He is not allowed to lie down on the floor. He may sit, stand, or walk around the house all he wants. However, he is not allowed to touch anything, including toys, objects on shelves, and so on. He is not allowed to go outside, take phone calls, play video games, read, or draw. He may go to the bathroom briefly, but he may not take a bath or shower. If meal time comes during Monster Time Out, the amount of time it takes to eat is added on to the end of the Monster Time Out period. Meals will be simple and will not include dessert. He will not be allowed to eat anything else during the four hours. If he has questions, he will be given only brief answers because no one is allowed to have conversations with him during Monster Time Out. In general, all he is allowed to do is walk quietly around inside the house, sit, or stand. This all adds up to being allowed to do nothing. The child will get intensely bored, which is the whole point (boredom of this magnitude is exceptionally aversive to children, and they will not soon forget about it).

Parents tell me that at first their children think Monster Time Out is a big joke. They can't see the punishment in such a situation.

However, after about an hour of having nothing to do but walk around quietly, or sit, or stand, and of having to leave any room in which anyone else wants to use a TV or stereo, they do indeed begin to get extremely bored. We sometimes forget that children's sense of time is quite different from that of an adult, and four hours to them seems endless. One ten-year-old told me that after two hours he was begging his parents to give him jobs to do because he could not stand doing nothing. One eleven-year-old told me that Monster Time Out was the worst punishment his parents had ever used, and he never wanted to go through it again.

In most cases restrictions such as these get the attention of even the most oppositional child or teenager when used frequently enough, consistently enough, and long enough. Don't forget that it is entirely possible for your child to have a Monster Time Out and to assume afterward it is safe to bring back the attitude. You may want to free her of this misconception by letting her know you are willing to give her back-to-back Monster Time Outs—something you would not wish on even your worst enemy. You may also let her know that if she begins to yell, argue, kick, or scream during Monster Time Out, you will reset the clock and let her start all over again.

With oppositional teenagers, it is possible you will be forced to remove their access to their obvious and subtle reinforcers for days on end. If you work outside the home and cannot be with your teenager to make sure he does not use the reinforcers available in your home while you are gone, let him know clearly that you will make sure he does not use them when you are home. Also let him know that things like computers, televisions, telephones, favorite articles of clothing, posters from his walls, CDs, tapes, and so on can be put in the trunk of your car or stored in a friend's basement until his behavior improves. If you want to get control of an oppositional teenager, you must be willing to go to these lengths. As I have said to many parents, you must be willing to devote your spare time to making the oppositional child miserable when reason and logic do not work and when the simpler forms of warnings and time out fail. It's sad but true, oppositional kids are often so busy making everyone else unhappy that they don't experience any lengthy periods of unhappiness themselves. Parents must often make them miserable before they finally gain some insight into how they make others feel.

Should the intense forms of time out fail, which is a possibility, there are yet other procedures to turn to. However, you should also be aware that there is something diagnostic about the fact that you have been forced to use these intense procedures and your child has still not shown indications of behavior change. Children and teenagers who remain strongly oppositional in the face of having their ability to move about and their access to their reinforcers so severely limited are special cases. They often have multiple problems. In addition to being oppositional and defiant, they may have learning difficulties or attention deficit hyperactivity disorder. They may be depressed, overly nervous, or overly anxious. They may have an antisocial personality style (a disturbance in their ability to interact with others cooperatively) of such magnitude that they will almost invariably come to the attention of the police and courts early in life. We will discuss these children in greater depth in a following section.

Level Systems

The next step up is typically known as a level system. In this system, there are multiple levels of access to reinforcers, with some levels being more restrictive than others. You may wish to use a system of three levels. I should also add that many parents who have used level systems in the past are turned off by the concept because it typically entails some sort of record keeping or charting to determine what level a child has attained. The system I will describe to you is more informal and requires no record keeping at all.

Explain to your child or teenager that, at the end of each day, you will briefly give him feedback on his behavior for that day. His performance today determines the level he starts on tomorrow. If he has demonstrated what you believe to be adequate behavior for the day, then the next day he will be on level III. If his behavior has been borderline or marginal, he will begin tomorrow on level II. If his behavior has been highly oppositional and unacceptable, he will begin tomorrow on level I.

The level your child is on determines how much or how little access he has to reinforcers. Someone on level III gets "usual" access to reinforcers (this system does not involve giving special rewards for good behavior, a practice I typically discourage). Being on level III does not mean your child gets to ride his bicycle all that he wants—he gets to ride it the amount usually allowed, which hopefully is based on reasonable and customary standards for children of similar ages. For example, if he usually gets to ride to your neighbor's house and is allowed to be gone for two hours, then that is what is allowed on level III. It is the same with any other reinforcers available. With teenagers, for example, if they normally get to use the Internet two hours a day, then that is what they get on level III.

On level II, everything is cut by at least two thirds. If your child normally gets to watch TV for two hours per day when his behavior has been good, when he is on level II he gets to watch for about a half hour. On level II, if kids are normally allowed to have company come over for two hours, they can stay for only a half hour. Phone calls are limited in number and should be brief. They can still go outside, but they must return quickly. On level II, kids are not allowed to go to someone else's home.

On level I, everything is taken away. Your child can do little else than read school books or a newspaper and hang around the house. Level I is something like being in Monster Time Out for an entire day, except reading educational material is allowed.

Here are the general ground rules for level systems: First, before a level system can be successfully employed, both parents and children must have a clear understanding of what the "usual" rules and standards of behavior are. All children need a secure sense of what is expected of them before they can be asked to alter their behavior. In short, we have returned to the concept we discussed in chapter 2: structure. Be sure you have addressed problems with this basic issue and have firmly established a consistent structure in the home before trying a level system. Using such a system arbitrarily or inconsistently will only engender further resentment and hostility. Second, don't move to something so intense as a level system until you are totally sure that the less intense procedures won't work. Level systems are not meant to be used for brief periods but for lengthy periods, such as one month or more. Discontinue use of the level system only after several weeks of continuous level III behavior and be prepared to reinstitute it if your child's behavior reverts.

When using a level system, be sure your child understands that although she might start the day at level III, she can be "busted" down to level II or even to level I, should her behavior warrant it. Once she moves down, she may not move back up. Although it would be tempting for her to throw a fit for the rest of the day, remind her that doing so only ensures she will start out the next day on a lower level. The child or teenager who contains herself for the rest of the day can begin the next day on level III again.

If you are forced to use a level system, you may find that your child will attempt to use it against you in some creative ways. She may spend most of the week on level II or level I, neither of which allows her to visit friends or to go out with friends. Then, come Friday, she may become miraculously good. After being moved up to level III on Saturday, she may expect to be allowed to go to the movies with her friends or hang out with her group at someone's house. Initially, at least, you need to allow her to get the benefits of level III. Maybe she will enjoy it enough to continue to strive to remain on it. If you find, however, that she keeps you miserable with her behavior all week long, then earns level III for Saturday by being good all of Friday, you need to have a clear discussion with her about her pattern. Let her know that you will make only a modified level III available to her if you see the pattern described. On this modified level III she gets to watch TV, take phone calls, and do most of her desired home activities. Her ability to leave the house alone or to go off with friends can be withheld until the weekdays go more smoothly. Be prepared for your teenager to argue with you that such an arrangement is not fair. Be prepared to inform her that it is also unfair that you have to put up with her oppositional behavior during the week and that you do not intend to make her weekends pleasant just because she managed to behave well for one day. Tell her that the behavior program she is on is yours, not hers, and you will set the guidelines for it. Tell her that while you will attempt to be fair, you have no intention of having your system used against you.

Pay-As-You-Go

There is one more level of intensity to move up to in the event your child or teenager does not respond to a level system. This is a short-term intervention, useful for only several days at a time because of the demands it places on the parent. I refer to this as pay-as-you-go. The premise of pay-as-you-go is that your child or teenager has failed to benefit from all of the other systems because he has not realized his reinforcers are connected directly to his behavior. With this last system, he will learn about this connection very quickly.

In a pay-as-you-go system, you start the day with zero access to reinforcers of any type, other than a basic breakfast and clothing. This is essentially different from all the other systems in that you are guaranteed nothing at the start of each day. At least Monster Time Out is over in four hours and you get back broad access to your stuff if you behave. You might spend a day on level I, but few people begin each day there. In pay-as-you-go, though, a child must demonstrate pleasant, cooperative behavior before he gets access to anything. For example, he would not be allowed to have that cup of hot chocolate he likes and watch the morning news without first demonstrating at least a half hour of pleasant, cooperative behavior. The rule is that he must be pleasant for thirty minutes before getting to do thirty minutes of desired activity. The entire time you are home is split into thirty minute blocks. If your child is pleasant and cooperative the first half of the hour, he gets to do what he wants for the second half of the hour. At the end of the hour he reports back in and then must spend the first half of the next hour being pleasant and cooperative prior to being allowed to go do more desired activities during the second half of the hour. If the parents do not judge his behavior during the first half of the hour to be pleasant and cooperative enough, then he spends the second half of the hour doing absolutely nothing.

"That's the stupidest thing I ever heard of," one exceptionally oppositional teenager told me as I was describing pay-as-you-go to his parents. I agreed with him entirely and pointed out that it is thoroughly stupid to behave in a way that is so bothersome to others that such drastic methods have to be used to make you act differently.

There are typically a number of other questions about the pay-as-you-go system. One teenager asked if she wanted to go out with her friends for a movie and pizza, could she demonstrate about four hours of good behavior first. I let her know that it was up to her parents to decide. One view is that for anyone to be placed on this system implies that her behavior is so bad in general that she should not be allowed to leave home at all. Others may counter that if she earns such a big block of time, it may reinforce better behavior. I have no problem with either viewpoint, with the provision that if your teenager is snarly and rotten all week, she will not be allowed to go out with her friends Saturday afternoon simply by being decent for a few hours that morning. Again, any system like this belongs to the parents, and they set all of the rules and the exceptions to the rules. It does not have to be fair. If the child or teenager had been fair to begin with, she would not be facing this situation in the first place.

PUNISHMENT SHOULD FIT THE CRIME—AND THE CHILD

Parents typically struggle with the idea of what is enough punishment for oppositional behavior and what is too much. There are no firm rules. Typically you judge your intervention by its success or lack thereof. In order to focus it a bit more finely than this, however, there are a number of considerations to keep in mind. For example, you should respond to your child or teenager in proportion to their oppositional behavior. If they are only mildly oppositional and seem to be doing it as a way to probe the limits and find out how the family structure is operating, then you would not respond with something so intense as a pay-as-you-go system or with Monster Time Out. Likewise, you should not expect a half hour in his room to make much of a dent in a fifth grader who curses at his teachers and assaults his peers on the bus.

Another important consideration is the child's age. In the next few sections, we'll explore the issues involved for dealing with oppositional children at different ages.

Young Children

Parents have a wide range of options to use with children who have not yet reached puberty. A child can be given time out in her room, time out sitting on a chair in the den, time out sitting on the stairs, and so on. If one spot doesn't work, try another. Remember, this is after you have used warnings and the warnings have failed. It's important young children understand that the point of time out is to sit and think about how their behavior got them in trouble and how to change their behavior. Let your child know that you will check on her while she is in time out, and if you find her playing with toys, the time out can start all over. You must be willing to do this for as long as it takes to get your child to follow your commands. If it takes two hours for your child to complete a ten-minute time out successfully, then that is what it takes.

If time out in the bedroom simply does not work for your youngster (don't try it once or twice and decide it doesn't work—try it on at least ten occasions), then try a chair in the den or kitchen or try sitting on the stairs or in the middle of the floor. I know one mother of a hyperactive oppositional child who had to resort to placing her son in a chair in the middle of a room so that he could not touch any objects. Otherwise, while doing time out at the kitchen table he would entertain himself by playing with the salt shaker. He made hats out of the newspaper while he sat on the couch in the den.

In some special situations it is important to be willing to restrain your child. I find that this works only with children ages four, five, and six, as the older children are so strong that they may hurt themselves while struggling with you. With young oppositional children who simply refuse to stay in the time-out chair, use a basket-wrap technique in which you sit in the chair and hold the child so that you are both facing the same direction. Take your right hand and hold your child's left wrist and do the same with your left hand and his right wrist. At first your child might think this is funny and is a game. After a few minutes the particularly strong-willed child may attempt to thrash around and escape. Be sure not to hold your face too closely to the back of his head, as he may, in his thrashing about, butt you in the face. You must remain calm while doing this, and it is important to continually whisper to your child that the time out will be over when you are satisfied with his behavior. In general, a minute or two of calm behavior should signal to you that you don't need to hold him any longer. Once he is calm and more willing to comply, let him know that he must sit quietly until time out is over. It is not uncommon at the end of this procedure for the child to be lathered with sweat, crying, and complaining. You should point out to him that you will use this technique only when he refuses to comply with your request to sit in time out. Let him know clearly, however, that you will use it as often as necessary.

If you find that using the strongest types of procedures are necessary and that your child is beginning to comply, let him know that you will soon give him a chance to use the less intense forms of time out. If he can be successful with the lesser forms, knowing that you will use the more intense forms if necessary, then he has learned a valuable lesson and you have saved yourself a considerable amount of grief and energy. At the same time, should time out in all of its forms fail to make an impact on your oppositional youngster, move to the level of combining time out with an hour's loss of access to several of his favorite activities or objects. Should this fail to get his attention, make the loss of access up to three hours. The key is to maintain your willingness to increase the intensity of punishment in small increments until you achieve behavior change.

Older Children

Kids ages eight, nine, and ten should likewise start with time out. When you initially punish these children, it usually takes them at least fifteen minutes to work through their fantasies of hating your guts and running away before they feel contrite. Again, follow the guidelines outlined for the younger children above, customizing them for older children. If twenty to thirty minutes of time out fails to get their attention and fails to help them modify their behavior, begin adding restrictions from reinforcers. These can range from mild restrictions to loss of access to all reinforcers, both obvious and subtle, for an entire morning, afternoon, or evening. If this fails, move to Monster Time Out and make sure that they get a true taste of boredom. If need be, you can move to a level system with them, or even to pay-as-you-go.

Tweeners

Once you get to ages eleven and twelve, you are in "tweener" territory: not a teenager yet but with decidedly different sensibilities than children just twelve months younger. These kids make up their own category emotionally. They have rightfully begun to demand more freedom and room but have yet to develop the oversensitivity to interacting with parents seen in thirteen- and fourteen-year-olds. The tweeners are the last age group for which I recommend using time out in the bedroom as a behavior-change tool. By the time they turn thirteen or fourteen they don't want to be anywhere close to you to begin with—they barricade themselves in their bedrooms on their own. Tweeners often still like being around adults, particularly if the adult is doing something they are interested in or if they consider the adult to be "cool." Time out in their rooms, away from the activity of the family, still gets to them. Use the same general guidelines explained so far. Try thirty minutes of time out. If oppositional behavior returns quickly, you've learned that time out alone does not work. Again, begin restricting reinforcers, increasing time out periods, etc. If you are willing to make them stick, these tactics will get their attention. This is, however, where most people fail with their oppositional tweeners. They will threaten catastrophic loss of all goodies for an entire day, then back down and let the child get away with little actual loss. Although you have no doubt heard this from every direction, let me say it again: Don't threaten anything you are not totally willing to do.

Early Teens

The ages of thirteen and fourteen are when most children enter the firm grip of raging hormones, although many girls are there a good year and a half in front of the boys. This is when they achieve the height to look most mothers and a few fathers in the eye, and this singular event whispers to them that they have finally achieved equality. However, this is a horrible time for them. Their bodies are sprouting hair and protuberances, and their voices are cracking. Their moods are about as stable as the San Andreas Fault. Their brains, however, have finally soaked up enough information and knowledge to use against you when they argue.

I typically refer to the age of fourteen as the "dead zone" because at that stage there is absolutely nothing parents can do to control oppositional teenagers as long as they depend on reason and logic. Using reason and logic on an oppositional fourteen-year-olds is like pouring water on a duck. Because their own ability to use logic has increased so much, they come to believe that adults who do not see issues the same way they do must be stupid.

As one mother told me about her fourteen-year-old son, "Here's the problem. He's too big to spank. If I were to hit him, he'd just laugh at me. When I take stuff away, he tells me he doesn't care. I don't have any power over him." Granted, it is hard to get the attention of oppositional fourteen-year-olds because this is the age at which they feel the most invincible. They can't date yet, so you don't have that to take away. They aren't old enough to drive or to take driving classes, so you can't threaten them with the loss of wheels. Most of them can't hold part-time jobs, so you can't take away an income source. If you tell them that they are limited for a night or two from the phone or TV, they will tell you convincingly that they don't care.

However, don't believe your thirteen- or fourteen-year-old when he tells you that he doesn't care if you take away his TV or phone privileges. Children in this age group fear boredom more than just about anything else. Also, as we discussed earlier, don't make the mistake of sending your child to his room. His room is where he wants to be. Instead of grounding him to his room, ground him from his room for two hours. Tell him that because of his attitude he has lost access to the phone, TV, and to his room. Tell him he has to sit in the den, the living room, or the kitchen. If he is in a room where someone wants to watch TV or listen to music, he has to leave and go find somewhere else to sit. Make sure he understands that because he will have to be around others while he is grounded from his room, he must be pleasant. If he is unpleasant, he should be grounded longer. It should not take all day to complete this time out, but it can if he takes you to the wall.

As with other age groups, if initial restrictions do not adequately get their attention, you must increase the intensity of the intervention. Children this age are particularly sensitive to restrictions from time with friends. These kids are unlike older teens in that they don't really own anything of real value because they are either not old enough or they haven't been able to do enough real work to buy the expensive stuff on their own. All they have are their attitudes and their stories gossip, and they have to be around peers to use either of these. Since their friends are their major reinforcers, making them stay home with you has a powerful effect.

Teens of Driving Age

The dead zone extends up to about age fifteen and a half, at which point whole new areas of leverage become available to parents. This is about the time teens begin to take driver education, and most children in this age group are keen on getting a driver's license. Once they are interested in driving, as the parent you are now back in business.

Every year a number of parents ask me if they should stop their children from taking driver education because of their behavior. I always suggest that they go right ahead and allow their children to complete driver training and get a license as soon as they can pass the test. Once they have completed all of these steps, they are so close to driving that they can almost taste it. The allure of being so close is precisely what you want working in your favor. Look at it this way: If you tell your teenager that she won't be able to drive and she has yet to complete driver ed, that is not a particularly potent threat. If she already has her license and you tell her that she is not allowed to use the family car until her behavior changes, then you have a powerful inducement in your hands.

You will find that most oppositional teenagers of driving age believe that driving is a privilege granted to them by the creator of the universe. If you make the mistake of allowing your oppositional teenager to buy his own car or if you make the mistake of actually giving an oppositional teenager a car, you will encounter strong resistance the first time you try to tell him that he cannot drive. You'll hear, "It's my car! I paid for it myself! You can't tell me I can't drive it! I'll get in it right now and leave and you better not get in my way!" And so on.

I have mixed feelings in general about teenagers owning cars. These feelings revolve primarily around the fact that academics often take a back seat to cars once the teenager thinks the car is his (I say "his" because this problem is mainly seen with males). Teenagers who own cars also often have to take part-time jobs to support the car, which also interferes with school and maintaining a normal social life.

I have watched too many teenagers choose between college and cars over the years. Typically, the choice begins somewhere around junior or senior year. The young man gets such an intense bug to own a car that he takes a part-time job, then has to work more to buy insurance, and has to work more to cover repairs. After all this working, there is no time left for school. To avoid this, I suggest that families who can afford it buy second cars and allow their teenagers to use them. It is important, though, to make it clear that the car belongs to the parents, not to the teenagers. When families can't afford extra cars I urge parents to allow their teenagers to use their vehicles on a reasonable schedule—one that won't disrupt the parents' lives but that will allow the teenager to engage in an adequate social life.

I tell oppositional children and their parents that the use of a car is only for individuals who have proven that they are capable of doing so wisely. Access to things that cost thousands of dollars is a perk that has to be earned, not granted simply because of age. To push this argument further, all of the things a family owns and uses should be seen as perks that have been earned.

The oppositional teenager in the age range of sixteen to eighteen is best dealt with by giving or removing access to life's perks and restoring access based on appropriate behavior. For this age, you must be willing to control access not only to large perks like cars but also to the small perks as well.

The ground rules for sixteen- to eighteen-year-olds are the same for the other age groups: begin with talk, move to warnings, then move to mild restrictions from reinforcers, and then on to intense loss of access to reinforcers. Somewhere along the way you will get their attention. But be prepared for a vigorous battle. Oppositional teens are hard-bitten with the notion that they are your equals and that no one has the right to tell them what to do. When pressed, they will admit they they depend on you for food, clothing, and shelter. In a way that defies logic, they still see themselves as your equal. This is likely based on the fact that they now look like your equal in terms of size and physical development. Also, many of them are able to hold their own in an argument without having to run out of the room and slam the door to prove you can't control them.

Given the physical size and maturity that goes along with this period, the late teens are often the most heartbreaking for the parents of oppositional and defiant children. You might be in the position of seeing your neighbor's seventeen- or eighteen-year-old achieve and earn trust and admiration as expected, while your own seems intent upon defying every rule written. Although it is sad to watch him act in such a self-defeating manner, it is nonetheless important to provide limits and punishments. Children in the late teens who are oppositional and defiant are incredibly capable of harming themselves and others. At the age where you had hoped you could begin to let go, you often have to take even more control.

CHAPTER SIX

After You Have Control: Training a Competent Child

I'VE HAD MANY oppositional children and teenagers accuse me of taking pleasure from designing ways their parents can punish them. As is typical, they operate from the viewpoint that adults somehow enjoy exercising coercive control over them. The interventions we have discussed thus far are in reality not fun for anyone. Their only purpose is to return control to the parents.

It may seem that gaining control of the situation is itself the desired goal, the end point. But the only purpose of interventions such as time outs, warnings, and level systems is to stabilize the situation. They are not curative, and they should not be the centerpiece of your long-term strategy of training your child to act in a competent, successful manner. Ideally, our children and teens should need less management as they age. The actual desired goal is for your child or teenager to move to a level of thinking and behavior in which minimal exercise of control over him is necessary.

My own parents were as fallible as anyone's, but they were absolute geniuses at granting freedom. When I turned sixteen and got my driver's license, I asked them what my curfew time was. They looked at me with the kindly bemusement that I remember so well from them and told me that I didn't have a curfew. They didn't really have to say anything else because their message was clear. They were telling me to make smart decisions. They were saying to me, in effect, "Don't make us take control of your life. If we have to, you won't like it."

LAYING THE FOUNDATIONS OF COMPETENT BEHAVIOR

We are obligated as parents to train children and teenagers in the beliefs, attitudes, and behaviors that will lead them to become competent individuals. By competent, I am describing individuals who generally operate toward the top of their ability level in whatever area you care to measure. They must make competent decisions about who to hang out with, about how hard to work at school, about how to interact with people. If a child has the potential to get As and Bs, doing so is evidence that they are acting in a competent manner. If their ability is limited to Cs, then making average grades also illustrates competency.

If we can assume for a moment that thinking influences behavior, then there are a number of thoughts that parents, children, and teenagers must embrace to achieve competence. These ideas need to be taught directly by the parents; they should become part of the family's philosophy of conduct. Without clear notions of what defines them as competent persons, children are likely to become the sorts of individuals who expect little of themselves and who offer nothing but excuses for their personal failures. Ideas that serve as the foundation of competent behavior follow.

Children Have Responsibility for Their Actions

On the surface of it, nothing seems more clear than the idea of personal responsibility. But it is also clear that many parents are willing to make too many excuses for their children. Teachers and school administrators encounter this all the time. They might place some form of restriction on a disruptive child, only to be confronted the next day by parents who believe their child is somehow being discriminated against or treated unfairly. I see it too frequently in my own office. There will be a weeping mother and a hulking, stone-faced adolescent. The mother will explain that Junior is really a good boy; it's those bad teachers who have it out for him. It usually turns out that Junior has been doing drugs since age fourteen and has a tendency to beat up anyone he doesn't like. Although it is true that many children have not been given a good chance in life because they've been raised by crazy parents or in crazy circumstances, isolating them from the consequences of their own behavior gives them no chance to learn how to be competent.

Parents Are the Ultimate Judges of the Child's Behavior

You will get a lot of argument from oppositional children and teenagers about this notion. Their positions revolve around ideas such as "no one has the right to tell anyone else how to act" and "it is not fair for one individual to judge another." Oppositional children generally want to go by standards that they themselves invent or by standards that are convenient at the moment.

Teenagers take their behavior cues from each other, although none of them will admit that they copy each other. A relatively recent teenage fad where I live, for example, has been growing goatees. It is not at all uncommon to see groups of five or six teenage males all sporting this look. I have pointed out, innocently enough, to several of the teenaged males I work with that this seems to be the new fad. They all deny that cultivating the hair on their chin has anything to do with what anyone else is doing. "I just don't like to shave," they all say.

Although it is harmless enough for children and teenagers to follow fads, believing that their behavior cannot be or should not be judged by their parents is a major error in thinking. It may lead to the assumption that their behavior should not be judged by anyone, which will leave them vastly disappointed once they begin to date, take jobs, or be in positions requiring cooperation with group members. They may become like the young woman who complained to me bitterly about her supervisor at the fast food restaurant where she worked. "She thinks she can tell me what to do," she said.

Children Must Learn to Anticipate Consequences

As we have said of oppositional and defiant children and teenagers, they fail to learn by experience. This is the reason you have to punish them over and over for the same things.

Learning to anticipate what might happen is a skill you have to teach your oppositional child or teenager because they probably will not come by it otherwise. Seemingly, once an idea crosses their mental register, they act on it. It feels terrifically important to tell their teachers to shut up the moment before they say the words, but they fail to think about what might happen after the words pop out.

With prepubescent children, I play a game called Time Machine, and with older children and teens I use the term "forward thinking." In the Time Machine game I ask the child to imagine he is getting ready to do something negative, something one of his parents has already told me they are prone to do. Then I ask him to imagine that just before he does it, he jumps into the time machine and goes forward ten minutes to see what might happen if he does. Children are almost always able to outline the negative outcome their behavior will precipitate. I ask parents to play this game frequently with their oppositional children so that the child can get used to anticipating outcomes.

The idea of forward thinking is the same, but without the game-like trappings used to engage younger children. I tell older children and teenagers that we all have negative or antisocial impulses we are tempted to act upon, and the difference between the person who stays in trouble and the one who stays out of trouble is that they learn to think forward in a way that lets them anticipate what the outcome will be.

It is important to let oppositional children and teenagers know that they are not the only ones who have antisocial ideas. It allows them to see that having such thoughts is quite normal. It also lets them see that the thoughts can be controlled, not translated into behavior that will cost them in the long run.

This would be a typical conversation I might have with a twelve-year-old whose mouth has kept her in trouble:

Me: "Let's suppose I'm sitting in the mall and I see some girl walking by with a two-foot high mohawk haircut that has been spray painted red, green, and purple. Why shouldn't I just say 'Hey, that's a really stupid haircut' when she walks by me?"

Her: "Because she might knock your face off."

Me: "That's true. She might also go complain to the security guards, who might have me removed from the mall. That would be embarrassing. The other thing is that it might hurt her feelings. Here she was minding her own business, and someone acted like a jerk toward her for no reason. She might have a funny haircut, but she could be an okay person. It's fine for me to privately think her hair looks funny. But the smart thing for me to do is keep my thoughts to myself."

Rewards Must Be Earned on the Basis of Performance

All kids like to bargain with their parents in the "if you let me do this now, I'll pay you back later," manner. Oppositional children seem to do it with more vigor and get more upset when you reject their promises. I met a fifteen-year-old a number of years ago who had his eye on a used Porsche. He told me that he had figured out a way to buy it. It involved having his father give him a two-year advance on his allowance, selling his stereo, TV, and baseball cards, and getting his mother, who was his custodial parent, to allow him to take a job bagging groceries thirty hours a week. He became incensed when his parents did not go for the deal.

I told him about another patient I had who was about his age. She was a Corvette fanatic who decided at the ripe old age of six that she was going to save her money and buy a Corvette when she got her driver's license. She got her parents to open a savings account for her and saved her allowance, gift money, and earnings from summer jobs for the next ten years. By the time she was sixteen she had managed to save enough to buy a clean, used Corvette.

Although I have already stated my reservations about kids owning cars, the point here should be clear. Oppositional children and teenagers want to be taken at their word but often fail to live up to it. They are prone to make promise after promise about doing better but fail to do so. They become angry when parents remind them of their promises and even more angry when parents attempt to tie access to their reinforcers to their actual performance.

In many ways, children and teenagers must be taught to be good capitalists. I often ask the oppositional children or teenagers how long they think their parents will have their jobs if they go to work and put their feet up and drink coffee all day. Even the most oppositional will respond "Not long." I then ask, if the parent loses his job, how long will he be able to have a car, a house, toys, and vacations? Again, the children always know the answer to this. When it is put in such terms, oppositional children and teens will grudgingly admit that they should not expect to get something for nothing in their own lives.

Rewards May Be Manipulated to Create Positive Behaviors

Parents always ask me if manipulating access to rewards isn't bribery. I always answer, "Of course it is." Although we hope that our oppositional children will change their behavior simply because it is the right thing to do, it is unlikely that such change will actually take place. In the field of psychology, arguments have been raging for decades about what causes behavior change. One side says insight causes change, while another says that increases or decreases in access to life's reinforcers causes change. Still another side says that learning to think in news ways causes change.

They are probably all right, but it is doubtful that any one view will be true for all populations. Highly ethical individuals who are concerned about how others think of them will probably use insight and examination of their own thinking processes to change behaviors that do not serve them or others well. With oppositional types, it is unlikely that you will get them to slow down long enough to examine their own behavior and thoughts until they are faced with the loss of their reinforcers. Manipulating their access to reinforcers, of course, should be teamed with a deep look at their behavior and a deep look at their ideas in order to effect lasting behavior change.

THE DEFINING OF COMPETENT AND APPROPRIATE BEHAVIOR

If you have a child or teenager who is highly oppositional, this next section is guaranteed to send them through the roof. They will maintain the belief that you cannot tell them how to live. The counter to this is that there are a number of life skills about which any parent has very clear expectations. You can indeed tell them how they have to live as long as they reside with you and depend upon you for all or most of their needs. The categories follow below, not necessarily in order of importance.

Attitude

Parents frequently ask me why their children and adolescents place so much importance on developing their in-your-face attitudes. The answer is deceptively simple. It is the only thing that they own. They are too young to vote or have real jobs, too young and poor to buy houses, and too powerless to have any real impact on their schools and government. Given that attitude is all that they own, it seems only natural that they spend time perfecting it. When your opposi-tional eleven-year-old looks at you and rolls his eyes after you have given him a command, you can bet that he's practiced this a hun-dred times, at least in his mind if not in front of his mirror.

When I ask oppositional children and teenagers if they have been whacking their parents with bad attitude lately, they almost always know what I mean. Our common language in this discussion revolves around behaviors such as open defiance, back-talking, dis-agreeing with anything anyone else says, pushing the limits too far, and so on.

I argue that parents have the right to demand that their children make themselves pleasant to be around. I am very unwilling to listen to arguments that such a demand somehow abridges children's rights or interferes with the expression of their indiviuality. If they are indeed simply being themselves when they are difficult to be around, then the best lesson they can learn is that large parts of who they are must be modified if they are to be successful in the broader culture. Not every behavior, personality pattern, or belief system is okay. There are certain attitudes and behaviors that will virtually doom you to failure, and being oppositionality is a main one.

There are many small skills necessary for projecting a pleasant attitude, including appropriate eye contact when talking or listening, managing nonverbal communications, and learning reciprocal verbal interaction patterns (psychologist mumbo jumbo for knowing how to hold a conversation with someone). We'll touch on each of these briefly.

Eye Contact

Oppositional children and teenagers will often purposefully avoid eye contact. I know one young man who is an absolute genius in the use of oppositional eye contact to disqualify or ignore everything his mother attempts to say to him. When she talks, he rolls his eyeballs upward so that all you can see are the whites of his eyes. At the same time he somehow makes his eyelids flutter and gets a sly grin on his face. His mother, stepfather, and I have all pointed out to him that this move almost defies human ability.

Teenagers have many reasons for using this type of eye contact (or none at all). Oddly enough, some of them tell me it makes them feel strange to make eye contact. Some will refuse to make eye contact as an expression of defiance and rejection of your authority, whereas others will stare at you without looking away as a sign of disrespect and an attempt to gain dominance over you through implied threat. Typically, the teenager who uses this method on adults is in vast trouble in most areas of his life, and teaching him better social skills will probably not help him solve his problems. He should be educated about the effect his staring has on others, but in my experience such teenagers already know what effect it has on others, and they find it desirable.

Two worlds collide over the issue of eye contact. Oppositional teenagers refuse to make it as a purposeful insult and a show of defiance. Adults demand it because it conveys respect and a willingness to engage in interpersonal interactions. In the adult world it is almost impossible to become successful in any job or career that involves dealing with others if you are not willing to make eye contact.

The ground rules for eye contact are relatively simple. Instruct your child or teenager that most people look directly into the eyes of the person they are talking to for about ten seconds before they look away to the side for a second or two. They then re-establish the contact and repeat the same pattern. Eye contact should also be punctuated by blinking. Otherwise it appears too intense. If your child or teenager is not comfortable making eye contact, have them sit in a chair across from you and practice doing it in the ten-second intervals described above. People who are averse to it at first will also find that after they do such an exercise repeatedly, making eye contact will become much easier to do. For children and teenagers who can make eye contact, but simply choose not to, you may wish to establish the rule in your home that you cannot hear them when they speak to you unless they make appropriate eye contact. Sometimes I ask young children to "Give me your eyeballs," when we are talking.

Nonverbal Communication

Other nonverbal communications that oppositional children and teenagers are prone to use are turning away from you or slouching while you are talking to them, rolling their eyes or making faces or exaggerated expressions while you are talking, making grunts, moans, or other noises while you are talking, or laughing derisively at much of what you say. The one thing all of these have in common is that when confronted with them, most oppositional children and teenagers will say "I didn't do anything." From their viewpoint, unless they have said something to you directly, or touched, grabbed, or hit you, they have done nothing. Although it can be quite interesting to listen to their rationalizations that their snorts, derisive laughter, and closed up body stance constitute "nothing," you can be certain that other adults find them every bit as irritating as you do. And once again it is here that the problem lies. Both parents and other adults in positions to help these children substantially are often unable to get past the negative messages they give off. Although it is well within human nature to want to help pleasant children or teenagers solve whatever problems they face, it's hard for adults to sustain their efforts to help the ones who are difficult to be around.

It is useful to role-play these negative behaviors for your preteen children so that they can see what they look like to others when engaged in high levels of oppositional nonverbal communication. If you decide to use this technique, do not exaggerate your role-play in a way that will deeply embarrass your child. Keep it as realistic as possible and then discuss with her what kinds of conclusions she would have made about you had you really been her age. Be sure to show her replacement nonverbal behaviors that she can use to make a more positive impression on others. I should note that this is not a technique that is likely to work with teenagers, because they are likely to conclude you are making fun of them. It is best to attempt to discuss it with them, perhaps through talking with them about the impressions they form of adults who display negative nonverbal behaviors toward them.

Verbal Reciprocation

Oppositional children and teenagers often have trouble with verbal communication as well. Reciprocal verbal interactions have their own set of hidden rules. For instance, what is your impression of someone who, when asked, "How are you?" answers only "Fine," without asking you how you are in return. Or, ask yourself what you think and feel about someone who talks only about himself and never asks questions about you. The old joke about these types goes something like this: "That's enough talk about me, let's talk about you. What do you think of me?"

Children and teenagers need to be taught two simple rules about talking with others. The first is that people who are judged positively by others tend to ask other people about themselves. The second rule is that real conversation requires self-disclosure, the act of saying something about one's own interests or ideas or accomplishments as they pertain to the topic of conversation. In my office I have children and teenagers who have underdeveloped social skills practice asking me three to four questions about whatever subject we might be talking about, then give one sentence about themselves before continuing. For example, a young man might ask:

"What kind of cars do you like?"

"I like sports cars," I would reply.

"What kinds?"

"Most Porsches and 1967 Corvette Stingray convertibles."

"Do you own either of those?"

"Not yet."

"I'm into trucks myself. I want to have a four-by-four one day."

This act of self-disclosure on his part sends a strong message. It says that he is taking the conversation seriously and that he is attempting to create a friendly atmosphere. It will make a positive impression on others, particularly if they are reciprocal individuals themselves.

Learning to Talk

Oppositional children and teenagers often don't know how to talk to other people. They clearly know how to defy and sometimes they know how to argue, but they often don't know how to state opinions that are not veiled put-downs, discuss issues, have friendly conversations, ask others about their lives, or disclose anything about themselves. It has been said that if the only tool you have is a hammer, you will treat everything like a nail. The same may be said for oppositional children. If the only type of verbal ability you have mastered is arguing, you are likely to argue with everyone over everything.

If you are the parent of such a child, you may be surprised to learn that he may not actually know what to talk to other people about, whether interacting with other peers or with adults. His storehouse of conversational topics might be empty. If he doesn't know what to talk to others about, your job is to help him make a list of topics and to then make sure that he has opportunities to practice on you and on others.

I use lists like the one you'll see in a moment primarily with prepubescent children. It should serve only to help you create your own list. Teenagers should be encouraged to do so too if they seem lost for subject matter. You can talk to others about where they live, what sports they like best, what sports they play, who their favorite celebrities are, where they like to go for pizza, their favorite subject in school, what they like to do when school is out, where they go to have fun with their friends, their favorite video game, the best movie they've ever seen, what movie they're hoping to see soon, where they want to go on vacation, their favorite brand of tennis shoe, and so on and so on.

I have seen some children become much less oppositional once they learn to talk to others. However, this takes coaching. You should sit down with your child and teach him how to use such a list. Some children will approach it quite concretely, asking one question about the first subject ("Where do you live?"), then move directly to the second subject ("What's your favorite sport?"), then on to the third, and so on, without going into any depth on any of the questions. Children who do this need you to practice with them by using role-play, making up a situation in which you pretend to be one of their peers or friends. Once they have begun to master making conversation with you, you need to make sure that you put them in situations where you can observe them interacting with other children. It is not sufficient to ask them whether they talked to someone at school that day, although you certainly will want to ask their teachers for such feedback. You must go with them to homes of friends, school outings, club meetings, sports practices, or other situations where you can directly observe their attempts to talk to others and give them gentle feedback on their progress. I have asked many parents in the past to go to their child's school during a recess period and observe from a distance (so the child doesn't know they're watching) how he interacts with others. Does he stand apart from others, not interacting? Does he interact by dominating, arguing, and bossing others around? Do other kids approach him and invite him to play? These are all things you need to know.

In general, having your child examine his verbal behavior and his nonverbal behavior will help him maximize his gains and minimize his losses. Although not a hard and fast rule, children with poor social skills are likely to get themselves into trouble more frequently than their more skilled peers, and they have fewer ways of getting themselves out of trouble than those same peers. The main reason they get in trouble more frequently is, without a doubt, their behavior. Nevertheless, others find it easier to dislike children who display poor social skills regardless of their behavior.

It is important to teach oppositional children and teenagers how to state their opinions without being offensive to others. I like to illustrate to them two basic roles they can take in conversations, the defensive and the nondefensive. In the defensive role they try to score points and win the argument. Although the defensive conversationalist may view the talk as a victory, from the perspective of the person attempting to talk to him (someone probably not even aware that he was engaged in an argument) he may simply seem inexplicably unpleasant and disagreeable. He is unlikely to try to talk to his oppositional acquaintance again.

This is how talks with oppositional children and teenagers go. You will be able to tell who is who:

Teen 1: "We're going to go Washington this weekend to see my grandmother. What are you doing?"

Teen 2: "Something a lot more fun than that. Family trips suck big time."

Teen 1: "I like going to see my grandmother; she's cool."

Teen 2: "She's probably lame."

And so on.

It is important to teach oppositional children and teens how to state an opinion nondefensively. In this role nothing is really up for grabs, there is no right or wrong position, and there is no winner. The point is to simply trade opinions so that each person gets to know the tastes and preferences of the other.

Psychologists who teach people to be more assertive often teach the technique of making an "I" statement. These are factual statements of opinion or desire. "I like sports cars better than pickups myself" or "I'd like to go to Hawaii instead of Alaska." The oppositional variant of both of these examples would be something like "I like sports cars. Pickups are for hicks" and "I'd go to Hawaii. You'd have to be stupid to choose Alaska." Although the oppositional child or teenager must be left to think this way if he pleases, it is the parent's job to make it clear that stating opinions this way will alienate him from others and will not be reinforced at home. A lack of conversational skills will keep such children from reaching competency in the interpersonal arena.

Have your oppositional child examine the statements above. Her task is to tell you which one is defensive and contains a "zinger," an implied put-down. Tell her that you will begin to let her know when her statements contain zingers and praise her for making statements that don't.

This can be quite a battle. Oppositional children or teenagers will insist that they have the right to say something is stupid if that is indeed their opinion. They are correct in a way. What they need to modify is how often they make such statements. Often everything that comes out of their mouths is negative or contains a zinger. Their initial goals should be to decrease the number of statements like these that they make daily and to become more aware that remaining highly defensive will drive others away. Don't buy into it at all when they say "Good, I want to drive everybody away." Such excuses just illustrate to you how trapped they are in their negative behavior and how they cannot yet figure out alternative ways of interacting.

Group Interaction

A powerful method for teaching positive interaction skills is to place your oppositional child or teen in group situations where it is necessary to give and accept appropriate feedback. Most oppositional types hate these situations. While in them they are often filled with fantasies of telling off the entire group or its dominant members. They do not readily think about how to become a member of the group.

Being in groups teaches your child or teen a number of things. The most important one is how to become "one of the guys." Not that becoming one of the guys is a skill that only males need to pick up. Being "one of the guys" simply implies that you are not brittle and rigid around others, as oppositional children usually are. Although they may become more at ease with themselves once they pass puberty, as children they are often tense and uncertain around other children, can't handle normal teasing when it is directed at them, and are only on familiar ground once they get an argument going. The problem with remaining brittle and rigid around others is that few of us have lives that allow us to work or live in total isolation. People who are otherwise capable but who do not know how to interact within a group often fail to achieve their potential.

Getting your child involved in groups is more simple than it may seem. Most schools have clubs of one sort or another that children can join. Most communities offer scouting, and most churches offer youth activity groups. Organizations such as the YMCA, YWCA, and the Boys and Girls Club often sponsor sports teams, as do county recreation departments and schools.

Your oppositional child or teenager will probably resist joining one of these groups. He will prefer either to be alone or with other like-minded sorts. It is important to have your oppositional child engage in group-based activities before she becomes old enough simply to refuse or to throw up such a gauntlet of negative behavior that you cannot get her to comply. It becomes almost impossible to force your child into groups at around age fourteen. I don't usually believe parents who tell me they cannot get their ten-year-old to go to basketball practice or Girl Scout meetings. I believe that they believe they cannot. The task is to prove to such a child that if she refuses to go along with the demand to get involved in group-based activities, she will have little to look forward to otherwise.

Once you have achieved a level of compliance that allows you to get your child to the group, make sure you stay and observe his interaction with the other members.

This is part of helping him become "one of the guys." Oppositional children and teens will initially hold back from interacting. Yours will need clear messages from you that he must try to act in a friendly manner, initiate conversations, use appropriate nonverbal communication, and participate in the task at hand. Make it clear that if he does not participate or if he acts in an oppositional manner, then the group is likely to give him some sort of negative feedback, such as rejecting him. Then he will have to work his way back into the good graces of the group. Quitting is not an option. You will know that you have achieved your goal as a parent when other children approach your own because they find him interesting and fun to talk to or when your child gets telephone calls from members of the group who want to talk or have him over for a visit.

Choosing Appropriate Friends

"You can't tell me who my friends are." You've heard this argument before, probably even used it yourself as a teenager. But suppose your child said to you, "You can't tell me I have to go to school." Chances are you would inform your child that as her parent you are obligated to see that she makes smart choices. It is the same with regard to choosing friends.

As I pointed out in the first chapter, oppositional children and teens take their social cues from their least successful peers. They are drawn to other oppositional children; everyone else is boring. I urge parents to meet the friends of their oppositional children and teens, either by having them come to your home or going where you can observe them. If you have younger children, ask their school to let you visit during lunch time, or when the kids can be observed on a playground. Observe without your child knowing so that you can see who he hangs out with. Do his friends tend to bully or intimidate? Do they stand aloof from group activities and sports? Does your child fail to interact with other children you know to be prosocial and successful, choosing instead to hang out with known troublemakers and peers who are failing academically and are disruptive to the learning process? If you can answer yes to any of these questions, you are well within your rights to insist that your child broaden his group of friends.

It is important that you not forbid him to see certain friends. Instead, emphasize that you want him simply to "broaden" his group of associates. This way you can escape his accusations that you are trying to control who he is friends with. It is virtually impossible to stop him from talking to his old, inappropriate friends on the playground or school bus, simply because you can't be there to stop it. But you can ask if he is beginning to play with other children, and you can verify this through his teachers or by returning to school and observing him again. Whether or not your child is making phone calls to set up activities with appropriate kids can also give you a clue, and you can monitor who is calling your child. It is also reasonable to ask your child's teacher to pair him up in work groups with prosocial children. Consider approaching his school counselor about having him join groups that could help him become more cooperative and friendly toward his peers.

When I mention these options to parents at lectures, there are always several who raise their hands and ask what can be done if their children simply refuse to do any of this on their own. In that case, all of the ideas we have covered thus far come back into play. First you attempt to talk to your child, using reason and logic about his peer choice. Should he reject reason and logic, you move on to warnings, at which time you point out what consequences you will provide if he continues to hang out with trouble-making peers. You may need to point out again and again that you own everything in the house, and if you are displeased with his peer choice you will be forced to restrict access to reinforcers to zero. Let him know that you will be willing to do this for as long as it takes. Also let him know that you will be willing to help him in any way necessary to find more appropriate friends, teach him the skills necessary to interact with nonoppositional peers, and so on. Your child must learn that you will not rest and he will not be happy until he makes good peer choices. But be sure also to tell him that after he begins to make better choices you will back off and allow him to manage his own social life.

These issues become a bit more complicated once your child is old enough to drive and has friends who also drive. You may find at that time that there is an explosion of kids who are new to you because they are all now mobile. Whereas your child previously tended to hang out with kids in the neighborhood and at school, now he can travel great distances to get to his new friends. Your position toward your child, if you know beyond a doubt that he tends to make poor peer choices, should be very clear: You are not allowed to get in a car with anyone until I meet him. If you are driving, I will expect you to drop by the house for a few minutes with your friends. If your friends are picking you up, I expect them to come inside and talk for awhile.

Of course you will not be able to pull this off perfectly. But stay insistent and meet as many of your child's friends as possible. Think of it as a sampling technique. No one who does public opinion surveys talks to one hundred percent of the people they are interested in studying. They talk to a sample and make conclusions based on the sample. But as any good researcher will tell you, the greater the percentage of the population you can talk to, the more accurate your conclusions are likely to be. Try to keep the percentage of your child's friends whom you have met relatively high.

If the results of your sample indicate that your child is hanging around with generally positive peers, ones who have good social skills and whose behavior and manner strike you as reasonable, then your child is probably on good ground. If your child comes in with peers who fail to make eye contact, mumble answers or respond to you with lots of I-don't-knows, who slouch or come into your home only partially dressed, or who wear drug or alcohol-oriented T-shirts, chances are you're in trouble.

Again, in lectures several parents usually raise their hands over this issue. "Isn't it possible," they ask, "that the ones who look like they have good social skills can be just as bad an influence as the other types?" The answer is a resounding yes, with an admission that there is only so much that we can know about a teen's true behavior pattern when they are away from us. But, in my experience, the ones with good social skills are less likely to get into serious trouble and are more likely to grow out of their oppositional ways as they age. It boils down to this: If I meet you and you reek of trouble by the way you carry yourself and interact with me, I will not reward my child for hanging around with you.

This is another point where parents ask questions. "What if you can't make your teenager stop hanging out with people who truly represent a danger to him?" This is a real push-come-to-shove sort of issue, but I believe that, if we err, it should be in the direction of overprotection, not the opposite.

I have any number of case examples of this sort of situation, but two in particular stand out. In the first, we have a single mother raising two daughters, ages fifteen and seventeen. The biological father was totally out of the picture except for signing a check once each month, and the mother had divorced a second husband who verged on being mentally ill. Although the girls had both experienced good relationships with their mother before the onslaught of puberty, the influence of their stepfather had soured them on adults in general. They began to hang out with other disenchanted teens, most of whom had juvenile arrest records, who were actively involved in alcohol and marijuana use, and whose lack of education, social skills, and grooming habits left them few prospects for the future. The mother would frequently come home from work to find the daughters with several of these friends.

As might be expected, the girls rejected their mother's attempts to talk about the sorts of people they were associating with. It became clear to her that talk would fail miserably in this situation. Both daughters began to skip school, gave every indication that they were using drugs, and began to mimic the snarly attitudes of the boys they were seeing. The boys were asked not to come to the house, but her daughters argued vociferously, "This is our house too. We have the right to have company." Given that she had to work, there was little she could do short of locking her daughters out every day until she got home, which was not an option. There were a number of other options, however, most of them radical.

Before I relate their story, let me offer a disclaimer. Parents should not move to radical solutions until all the other options we have discussed have been exhausted. It is guaranteed to alienate a teenager who may respond to lesser interventions. In this case, the mother had tried all of the traditional methods, from controlling access to reinforcers while she was home to removing driving privileges for the oldest girl.

I suggested, after the failure of all sensible options, that she begin to gather information on all of the people her daughters associated with. Although the police will not make formal statements, some officers are willing to tell you off the record whether someone is known to them. I told her that it was okay to ask each of the people who came to her house whether they had a juvenile or adult court record, had ever been arrested, or had ever been on probation, and why. Additionally, I told her to ask them whether they had ever been in treatment for substance abuse or had ever been hospitalized in a psychiatric hospital. Do they carry any weapons, such as guns or a knives? Do they have a history of shoplifting, breaking and entering, or stealing of any sort? Have they been expelled from school or do they attend an alternative school due to behavior problems? Do they have a history of assaulting their teachers or destroying school property?

I told her to write up a release of information form that her daughters' friends would be asked to sign so that she could get information on them from their probation officers and the police. This was a ploy, of course—no agency would ever consider releasing information to her. The juvenile delinquents didn't know that, however. I also told her she should consider having the ones who were known thieves to bring a fifty-dollar deposit with them every time they came to her home. If nothing was missing when they left, she would be more than happy to refund it, minus any charges for anything they may have had to eat or drink while they were there and minus what she would charge them if she had to clean up after them once they left.

Her first response was that these suggestions were all crazy. I indicated to her that the whole point was to give these young men the impression that she was indeed crazy. It would force them to weigh the trouble she might cause them against whatever reinforcement they got from seeing her girls, and they might choose to disappear.

The mom took my advice and things began to get better. The mother's requests for release of information and security deposits made the young men rather nervous. Her demands for information on one young man in particular turned up that he had been in a juvenile home because of numerous breaking and entering charges. She found this out by calling his mother and simply asking. Once her daughters learned of this, they began to cool their relationship with him because he had lied to them and to their mother when she had asked him point blank if he had an arrest record. They were beginning to open their eyes to the true nature of the young men they were attracted to.

In the second case, we have a basically good but mildly oppositional seventeen-year-old male, who had begun to hang out with boys several years older and who were known to be dealing small amounts of marijuana. His parents complained to me that there had been an increase in phone calls to their home from people they did not know and that there had been a drop in his contact with his old friends, most of whom they approved of. When the new friends came over to pick him up, the parents insisted on meeting them. They were nineteen to twenty-one years old with the gruff mannerisms and condescending attitudes that many undersocialized sociopaths display when they think you are not on to them.

I suggested that the next time the new friends came over, the father ask for the keys to the car they were driving. He was to explain to them that he was considerably worried about the issue of drug and alcohol use among teenagers and that he intended to search the car for seeds, stems, marijuana roaches (partially smoked marijuana cigarettes), beer cans, and so on. The father managed to rattle the new friends enough that they saw his son as a liability and faded out of his life rapidly. The son groused and complained, but the parents achieved their goal, which was to disrupt the relationship with dangerous peers.

Be careful about using these methods. Not everyone who looks different from you is bad, and you should not immediately place negative judgments on anyone who is not in your same social class, ethnic group, religion, and so on. American families have a history of doing exactly this, and it is hurtful to innocent people. At the same time, if you believe beyond reasonable doubt that the people your child or teenager is gravitating toward are dangerous to him or to her, do not hesitate to begin to disrupt the friendships.

Controlled Substances

You may find it disheartening that your teenager cannot go any place where there are going to be other teenagers and not encounter cigarettes, alcohol, and street drugs. Virtually every teenager I work with tells me this is so. Because of this, I believe children and teens need a rigorous education about the various substances, their dangers, and their long-term implications. Competency regarding the subject of drugs means acting toward controlled substances in a thoughtful, educated manner. This happens through family discussions, school programs, and reading. It does not happen in a one-time talk, like the one most of us were given about sex by a nervous parent. Educating your children about substances should be an ongoing effort, done in an interesting and informative way. But I must caution you, if you smoke, it does little good to tell your children not to. And if they see you drink to intoxication, they are going to pick up the idea that there must be something fun about it and set out to get drunk themselves. If you use street drugs, they will assume that there must not really be anything wrong with them and will want to try them too.

Even your best efforts at education may be defeated by the influence of your child's peer group. His teenage years are dominated by the tensions between how he has been taught to act by his parents and how he is being influenced to act by his friends. You have little chance of influencing the outcome of this struggle if you wait until he is already a teenager to talk to him clearly about the types of choices he will be faced with regarding substances, or if you yourself provide a bad example.

I try to tell parents that it is no disaster if their teenager sneaks a cigarette, drinks a beer, or tries marijuana in safe circumstances. I have yet to meet one generation who, as teenagers, did not attempt to sample controlled substances. Try to see such experimentation as an opportunity to have open, serious discussions about controlled substances. The disaster comes if the parents fail to talk, or if they react so outrageously that their teenagers learn it is safer to keep their mouths shut rather than to ask questions or admit having tried susbstances. If your teenager does decide to get drunk or get stoned, you want her to trust you enough to call you to come get her. You also want her to know enough not to do something truly foolish, like drive cars, go swimming, climb water towers with her friends, go drag racing, and so on. Make sure that you talk to your child or teen frequently about substances, and make sure you tell her you will never punish her if she calls you to come get her because she is too intoxicated or incapacitated to get home on her own.

Most substance-related disasters begin when teenagers make substances the center of their entertainment. You can blame this on their peers, but the truth is they have powerful social influences telling them how to regard drugs and alcohol, influences that have been giving them this message insidiously for years through commercials. It never fails to strike me as perverse when I see teenagers wearing T-shirts and hats that display the names of beer or cigarette makers. Part of your child's early education should be about the fact that there are huge corporations whose existence depends on inducing teenagers to use addictive substances.

Teenagers know exactly what I'm talking about when I ask them if beer or marijuana is at the center of their fun. For many of them, fun cannot be had without beer, marijuana, or cigarettes. To be more precise, teenagers often believe nothing can be fun unless they become totally wasted. "We don't know we're having fun until we puke."

To prevent such an outcome, it is important that children be taught how to to have fun early in life and encouraged to pursue it through activities such as sports and outdoor activities, reading, artistic endeavors, clubs and organizations, and the like. This is impossible unless children see parents pursue their own fun through these methods and unless parents pursue this way together with children. My sons are not likely to believe that hiking is more fun than sitting in front of a TV drinking beer unless I take them hiking.

We must take the position with our children and teens that competent behavior does not include having substances at the center of their lives. There are many arguments to be made that alcohol, beer, and wine are essentially harmless if used in moderation as an adult. This seems like a reasonable position as long as the family members who are saying such things are also living by them.

There will unfortunately be cases in which all of our talking and modeling moderation will not prevent our teenagers from focusing their lives around drugs and alcohol. It is at this point that strong action is called for. Given that oppositional and defiant teenagers are prime candidates for substance abuse, we need to let them know that using drugs regularly will result in other losses. If I know for a fact that my teenager is an active user of alcohol or marijuana, it would be foolish of me to allow him to drive or to hang out with the people he uses with. He should not be surprised when I take him for treatment. He should not expect that I will allow him to leave home alone or hang out with people I don't know. I believe that we must make it clear to teenagers that their most valued freedoms—the right to leave the house and the right to hang out with their friends—will be restricted until we believe they are substance free.

There are two issues that should be made clear to teenagers who use substances. First, if they are using drugs, chances are they are keeping them in their rooms or elsewhere in your house. Teenagers who are using are notoriously jumpy about you going into their rooms, and they will argue that they have a right to privacy. My own response is that competent teenagers do indeed have the right to privacy. There is no reason for a parent to search a teenager's room or go poking about in their things unless they have clear suspicion or evidence of substance abuse. Privacy goes out the window once behavior enters the drug zone. A competent parent will let the abusing teenager know that his room will be searched and any substances found will be destroyed. Searches will continue until the parent is satisfied that the teenager is drug free. The teenager should also know that the parent can elect to have random urine testing done at his doctor's office to determine whether substances are still being used.

Secondly, if your teenager is using substances, chances are he is using with his friends. When I believe this to be the case I ask parents to contact the parents of their teen's closest friends and alert them to the fact that drugs or alcohol have invaded the peer group. I suggest that parents convene a meeting with all of the teenagers present to confront the group on their substance use. Such meetings often last several hours and can be emotionally charged. It is vital that the parents not get pitted against one another, which can be difficult if it turns out that one of the teenagers is selling drugs to the others. The parents should tell the teenagers that appropriate treatment will be sought for them and that the parents reserve the right to hold future meetings.

I have frequently been asked if the purpose of such a meeting should be to break up the friendships between the teenagers. It depends on the situation. If your teenager is friends with another who is generally appropriate, displays good social skills, seems to be trying to do his or her best in school, and who isn't a thief, sociopath, or danger to your child, then you are probably better off allowing the friendship to continue after the parent meeting. At that point all the teens know they are being watched by an entire group of parents, and there is much positive that can come from this. However, I remain an advocate for disrupting relationships with dangerous peers.

Although all of this may sound extreme to your teenager, he should continue to be told that once he has begun to display competent behavior in general, which includes not being substance dependent or abusive, then the restrictions on him will decrease and his freedoms will return. Make it clear, however, that this will not occur until you are satisfied that he is making smart decisions.

Truthfulness, Lying, and Empathy

Oppositional and defiant children and teens can develop varying relationships with the truth. Many who will get in an authority's face in an instant will nevertheless do their best to tell the truth as a point of pride. Others will use the truth in a hurtful, aggressive way while they are operating in oppositional mode. I know still others who frequently lie. The oppositional child, as we have said before, always goes to the extreme. Instead of trying to wound you with the truth, she will try to chop your head off with it. If she lies, she tells whoppers.

I find that children who use the truth aggressively, or who lie, rarely have an understanding of how they make others feel. One of the aspects of becoming a competent individual is to become aware of the impact you have on others, particularly when it is negative. This is one of the more difficult tasks facing any of us in life.

Psychologists refer to this awareness of what others are feeling as empathy, and oppositional individuals often suffer from a lack of it. There is no way to teach someone how to think empathetically without first training them in the language of feelings and emotions. The first understanding my own children had about the nature of my work was that "Dad works with people who are either mad, sad, or glad." To this basic list you might add anger, guilt (feeling bad about something you did), shame (feeling bad about who you are), disappointment, and fear.

Teach younger children to analyze these emotions in others by role-play. During the role-play, make sure you get exaggerated looks on your face that the child has to analyze. With those who have hit puberty, ask them to analyze what someone they can observe might be feeling. It could be someone you're watching on television, or it could be a friend they talked to earlier. Your questions would revolve around identifying the basic emotions they are undergoing, as well as the intensity of those emotions. It might go like this:

Parent: "Look at that guy on the news. What do you think he's feeling?"

Child: "I don't know."

Parent: "We don't accept 'I don't know' as an answer around here. Look at his face and listen to his words and tell me what you think he's feeling."

Child: "He's talking about his car being stolen."

Parent: "How is he feeling about his car being stolen?"

Child: "I don't know."

Parent: "Remember that list of feelings we talked about. Sad, mad, glad. Anger, guilt, shame. Disappointment and fear."

Child: "He just said he was the one who left the keys in it."

Parent: "So what do you think he might be feeling. What would you be feeling if you left the keys in your car and it got stolen?"

Child: "I'd be feeling pretty sad."

Parent: "What else?"

Child: "Guilty."

You might find that it takes quite a while to get your oppositional child interested in this. The sad fact here is that the more oppositional your child, the less likely he is to care what someone else is feeling. You have to consistently point out to him that lots of successful people seem to have this ability, and most unsuccessful people don't seem to have it at all..

Once he has begun to pick up the simple terms outlined above, have him analyze how he is making you feel the next time he acts toward you in a highly oppositional manner. Again, it might go something like this:

Parent: "What do you think you made me feel when you told me I'm stupid?"

Child: "I don't know."

Parent: "Let me point out that it is dangerous to your freedom and privileges to not think at a time like this."

Child: "You felt mad?"

Parent: "How mad?"

Child: "Really mad?"

Parent: "That's right. What else am I feeling?"

Child: "Disappointed?"

Parent: "Why?"

Child: "Because it made you sad and angry when I talked to you like that."

Parent: "So what should you do?"

Child: "I guess I ought to stop."

Parent: "That would be smart. It would be even smarter for you to stop and think next time, 'What's Dad going to feel like if I whack him with attitude?'"

As in all cases, times may come when talk fails. Then you move to more drastic measures. My favorite intervention with children who continue to lie after ample discussion of feelings and empathy is to assume that everything the child or teenager says for the next twenty-four hours is a lie. This always sounds like fun at first to oppositional children, particularly the ones who have yet to reach puberty. They think of it as some big, silly game. But this is how it works:

Child: "Mom, I'm hungry."

Mom: "No you're not. You're lying again."

Child: "I am not. I need something to eat."

Mom: "What is it you want?"

Child: "I want a sandwich."

Mom: "I don't believe you. I don't think you really like sandwiches."

Of course somewhere in here you give your child something to eat, but certainly not anything that she asked for. The purpose of this intervention is to give her a taste of the type of frustration she makes everyone else feel with her lying and dishonesty. It sometimes takes shock therapy such as this to get the oppositional child or teenager to understand how they affect others. After you have your child's attention, return to the empathy training we outlined above. Let them know that you much prefer teaching them to understand their impact on others over punishing them with such drastic and ridiculous measures.

Stealing

Before I outline the simple approach I recommend for children with stealing problems, I want to make sure we've identified our terms. Many children will take a pack of gum from a store when they're young. If handled gently but firmly, such as by having them return to the store to return the item, it probably won't happen again, and won't constitute a problem with stealing. Some individuals steal compulsively because it satisfies a sense of anger and frustration, typically aimed at a parent who they believe did not offer sufficient nurturance during childhood. This is a deep-seated psychological problem and should not be seen in the same light as the teenager who goes to the mall to steal clothes that they intend to use or sell or who breaks into cars in search of stereos, speakers, or other valuables.

It is important for us to train our children that stealing is wrong. If they steal anyway they do not need lengthy explanations about why it was wrong, and they do not need us to make excuses for them. Many teenagers tell me that they stole because of the influence of a friend. However, when I ask whether they knew stealing was wrong, they always tell me they did. You would have to be either mentally deficient or raised by wolves not to know this by the time you are able to plan the theft of an item of any real worth. Because of this, I am not willing to accept excuses about stealing. I am willing only to accept admissions of responsibility, which should include a clear awareness of the need to change and the need to no longer associate with people who steal.

The fastest way to make an impact on the child or teen's stealing problem is through her own reputation. If you ask a child or teenager who has stolen if she considers herself to be a thief, you will almost always get a strong response, "No!" I like to ask unanswerable questions to make them think about their behavior, such as "How long can a nonthief do the things thieves do, and still not be considered a thief?" or "If you shoplift once, but don't consider yourself to be a thief, how many times would you have to shoplift before you do consider yourself to be a thief?"

Although such methods might seem harsh, I believe that stealing is one of the few problems for which it is appropriate to tap the sense of guilt and shame that most children and teenagers have inside. This allows their conscience to come to the front, where it is less likely to be pushed away the next time opportunity knocks. It is important for them to develop a way of thinking in which they say to themselves "I did something very wrong. I will not do it again."

But what if they continue to steal? After all, many of the teenagers I work with go with their friends to the mall with the intent of shoplifting. They brag to each other about how much they can steal in a given night. They consider it a sport, and even have names for it. In my area, some the the teenage girls refer to shoplifting as "racking," a term which, like most rationalizations, takes away the criminal aspects of the behavior. So, what if they refuse to remove themselves from relationships with peers who steal, or if they continue to steal themselves?

I believe in strong medicine for this. Children and teenagers who steal repeatedly, whether from a store or from acquaintances, often have no idea what it feels like to have something they love or value taken from them behind their back. They are unaware of the feeling of violation experienced by a victim of theft. Once it is clear that your child is going to continue to steal, explain that it is important for her to learn how bad she makes others feel by stealing from them. There is only one way for her to learn this, and this is from experience. Tell her that within the next few days to few weeks you intend to go into her room while she is out, and take something that she values. Let her know that once you take it, there is absolutely no possibility that it will return. Let her know that it will be senseless for her to accuse you of stealing the item, even though she knows it is you who took it. Tell her that you will deny having taken it, just like she has denied taking things from others. Let her know that she will find this extremely frustrating, and that this is your goal. Be clear that if she sees the loss of her valued object as a chance to get revenge on you, she will be placed on a level system and forced to earn everything.

Secondly, explain that because she has been identified as a thief, she now has the difficult task of rehabilitating her reputation. Let her know that she will find this frustrating as well, because she will believe that she can be trusted again before other people have come to that same belief. Imagine working hard and confronting yourself until you have become honest but then realizing that no one believes you. This is the frustrating point that all identified liars and thieves must work through, and it is not a position that you want to place yourself in voluntarily by stealing and lying.

Conspiracy Thinking

Oppositional children are often defensive and prickly. If you get angry at them for being oppositional, they may believe that you are acting this way because you are out to get them. They consistently fail to see that it is their own behavior that has made you or others mad.

The greatest obstacle to eliminating conspiracy thinking is often the parent. I should point out that it is entirely natural for children to operate on a conspiracy-based, paranoid logic during a certain period of their development. Their brains are not sophisticated enough to develop complicated explanations for their interactions with others. Given the human need to have an explanation for the cause of events, they move to simple answers. Bobby is mad at me because he doesn't like me. Suzy won't play with me because she's stuck-up.

I encounter parents weekly who are themselves still mired in this type of thinking, and it seems natural to argue that they unknowingly pass it along to their children. I had a conversation with a mother in the past few days who told me that the school system has it out for her son. I asked her what had happened. She told me that her son, who is eleven years old and was present at the interview, had been suspended for ten days. I asked what he did. She said initially that she didn't know, which struck me as remarkable in itself. If my kids were ever to be suspended from school, I would demand a clear explanation of what had happened, who was involved, and so on.

I asked the child what happened. He said that the teacher had told him to stop talking and that, when he refused, she asked him why he was still talking. He said to her "Because I want to," after which he was suspended for ten days.

I found such a reason to be unlikely. I explained it this way: If I was a child in this boy's same room, and the teachers had found me to be cooperative, hard-working, and not generally disruptive, then it is highly unlikely that I would be suspended for ten days for making one mildly oppositional comment. I might have spent the afternoon in the principal's office, but ten days suspension would be unheard of. If, however, I was the type of kid who had been oppositional and mouthy to my teachers for some time and I had developed a reputation for being bad tempered or hard to deal with, then sooner or later I was bound to place that final straw on the camel's back. At that time breathtaking consequences might indeed tumble down upon me. And, like most conspiracy thinkers, I would then complain that they were out to get me.

The more I probed, the more evidence I found of a lengthy history of oppositional behavior in school. The mother finally admitted that she had been overly protective of her son for years and had interfered every time the school system had attempted to provide consequences for his behavior.

The way around situations such as this involves several steps. If this pattern seems familiar, you must search yourself. If you find that you experience high levels of conflict or problems with others or with systems such as schools, courts, or other organizations, and if it seems to you that you are never to blame, then chances are you are a conspiracy thinker yourself. You need to ask yourself what it will mean to you to experience your own fault in matters. Will it make you feel like a failure to admit you have done things wrong? Will it make you feel dumb to admit to mistakes in how you have dealt with others? If so, then you need to understand that extremely harsh judgments of one's self make it next to impossible to deal with the truth. If I end up hating myself because I have made mistakes, there is little chance that I will confront myself. It is much better to face your mistakes calmly, rationally, and with a commitment to change.

You also need to determine whether your children or teenagers are so harsh on themselves, or so psychologically defended, that they cannot admit to mistakes. If their style of admission tends to be along the lines of "Okay, I hope you're happy; you've proved I'm stupid!" then you know they are overly defended and too psychologically brittle to deal with the reality of their own behavior. Such children typically have deeper self-concept issues and should be seen by a professional child therapist.

At the same time, you won't find a therapist who is willing to come live with you, so you've also got to learn to deal with your child's conspiracy thinking as it happens. When a conspiracy-prone child or adolescent says that her teachers, friends, or classmates are mad at her for no reason, gently inquire if it might be related to something she has said or done. Go easy here, out of an awareness that conspiracy thinkers and paranoids are quite brittle. When you reject their conspiracy explanation, they experience it as you reject-ing them, pitting yourself against them. At the same time, it is neces-sary to point out to conspiracy-prone children that they often blame things on everyone else, and this is not generally how things work. Explain to them that mistakes are human and that admitting to them helps us see more clearly how not to continue to make the same mistake over and over. You will find that some children and teens are not easily led to this type of insight because they have so much invested in being faultless. With these children and teens you have little alternative but to remind them that you are not willing to listen solely to conspiracy-based theories of their conflict with others. Require them to provide you with an alternative explanation. This will be difficult for them, so be sure to praise and reinforce them when they make an effort to explain things in a manner that exam-ines their own contributions. Acknowledge that it is hard and that you are proud of them for trying to get past the "nobody loves me, everybody hates me, I'm going to eat some worms" sort of thinking.

Use of Rationalization When Failing

Rationalization is something like conspiracy thinking; it is another attempt to avoid personal responsibility. The difference is that in rationalization the reason for failure is not that others are out to get you. It is that circumstances beyond your control have prevented you from living up to a responsibility. We all recognize these exam-ples because we have all used them ourselves. I couldn't finish my homework because my baby sister was crying too loud last night. I didn't get here on time because I was talking to my neighbor on the phone and couldn't get him to shut up.

It does not strike me that oppositional types necessarily use this defense more so than other children or teens. The reason it is bothersome when they use it is that they use it in addition to all of the other things they do that bug you. We may find ourselves accepting an excuse from a child or teenager who is not oppositional, but we may be totally unwilling to accept the same excuse from an oppositional child.

Oppositional children and teenagers must be trained not to make excuses just the same way other children are trained not to. This happens when they encounter disapproval and consequences when they do not live up to their commitments. Like all children, they must be taught to take responsibility for their failures, unless the circumstances were truly daunting. Another problem is that they are often aware that other children are given slack, so to speak, that they themselves are not given when they make similar mistakes. It is important to help them distinguish between their overall behavior patterns and the behavior patterns of others who get breaks from adults. They will not like this sort of direct comparison, but it will provide them with a realistic explanation about why others can sometimes get away with excuses while they can't.

Living Up to Academic Potential

This strikes me as one of the more important categories of competency. Children and teenagers must be taught that they have to live up to their academic potential and that there are few excuses for not doing so. If they are capable of work in the A and B range, then they should know that you will not accept grades in the C, D, or F range. If they are capable of getting grades in the C range and are doing so, then you will be pleased.

Although it is true that much of what our children learn in school will be forgotten, the benefit of school is that it teaches critical thinking skills, such as how to use information to solve problems or reach goals and how to get the most out of one's own abilities. Because they are unlikely to find a job that does not require them to think, use information, or try hard, it is best to learn these abilities and attitudes early in life.

Access to reinforcers should be tied directly to a child's academic performance, which includes their ability to work cooperatively with teachers, staff, and fellow students. If a child is experiencing academic difficulty due to home circumstances or psychological problems such as depression, anxiety disorders, or attention difficulties, it is incumbent on the parent to get the appropriate help for the child and to inform the school of the reasons behind his academic problems. Children who have real reasons for academic difficulty should never be punished for poor grades. It is only children and adolescents who have decided that they don't need or want to perform that I am concerned with here. To clarify, although I do consider poor attitude and behavior to be psychological issues, I do not see them as the types of psychological issues that exempt the children or teenagers from punishment.

I met a young man some time back whose name was Paul. He was pleasant and obviously smart. He had no history of academic failure up until the time he got to the tenth grade, at which point his grades went from mainly Bs to mainly Ds, with an occasional F. He explained that he had decided that since he was going to be a teenager only once, it was important to "enjoy" his teenage years. This precluded doing anything so mundane as homework. What really made him happy was renting movies to watch on his VCR on the days he decided not to go to school, shooting pool with his friends, and going to hockey games and football games on the weekends.

Paul was one of those kids who breaks your heart as a psychologist. You can see all the potential in the world in him accompanied by no desire to use it to become educated or trained in anything. Although he hoped to become a sports broadcaster one day, he made no connection between going to school, performing highly, and eventually getting such a job.

Kids like Paul are also fun to work with because they are friendly, have excellent social skills, and are bright. I remain optimistic about them, hoping that their personality style, social skills, and native intellect can carry them through. What is more likely, however, is that these types get hired because they are initially impressive but fired quickly once it becomes apparent that the attractive package has nothing inside.

In Paul's case, all I could do ultimately was recommend to his mother that she make his access to everything except the essentials contingent on going to school and working up to his potential. She could not be home during the day due to her work, and it was highly likely that Paul would skip school on certain days and stay home and enjoy himself. I asked her to control only what she could control. Given that she could be home only in the evenings, I recommended she devote her evenings to making sure Paul had access to nothing. He would be allowed to read academic books, and that was it. No TV, headphones, stereo, VCR. No phone calls. No going out anywhere with anyone. No access to snack foods, soft drinks, and so on. No long showers, no long baths. Her job was to show him that her response to his refusal to go to school or work up to his ability would be as radical as his decision that he should use his teenage years only for enjoyment. She was to let him know that enjoyment would come through demonstrated competence and not by any other route.

It is not often easy to find out how your child or teenager is doing in school. In fact, many parents tell me that they go along, thinking their child is doing just fine, then at the end of the semester they get their children's report cards with all sorts of negative comments about their performance, attitude, or behavior. If you have a child who is not performing up to his level of competency and you want to have him live by the notion that his access to his reinforcers is contingent upon his school success, then you cannot afford to wait until the end of the semester to find out how he is doing. The solution is to have your child or teen bring home each day feedback sheets that have been filled out by his teachers.

Let me lay out the ground rules. First, teachers are already burdened with enough paper work, so do not ask or expect them to fill out any elaborate rating sheet on your child. The sheets that I use have been designed to allow the teacher to fill them out in about ten seconds, literally. I do not ask for comments. Many teachers are often kind enough to make comments on the sheets, but it is not necessary in order for you to get the information you need.

Second, the child or teenager is responsible for taking the sheet(s) to school and bringing them home each day. If he fails to bring them to you for any reason, you should respond by assuming that the ratings were all bad and act accordingly.

Finally, the teacher's rating of his behavior in the classroom is the final word. No explanations or excuses will be accepted unless your child can truly prove extenuating circumstances. If he tells you a story that leads you to go so far as to call his teacher, only to find out that his story is essentially a crock, you must respond strongly enough to prevent him from making up lies in the future. Below you'll find a typical feedback sheet for a child whose main problems are negative behavior in the classroom and failure to live up to his academic potential.

DAILY FEEDBACK SHEET FOR (YOUR CHILD'S NAME)

Day of Week: M T W TH F   DATE:

	GREAT JOB	OKAY	NEEDS WORK
Did not disrupt others	____	____	____
Acted in a cooperative manner	____	____	____
Handed in any assignments due	____	____	____
Appeared to pay attention	____	____	____

Signature_____

If your oppositional, defiant child comes home with marks primarily in the Great Job and Okay categories, you should congratulate him on having a good day at school and allow him access to most of his reinforcers for that afternoon and evening. However, two to three Needs Work marks out of a possibility of four means that his reinforcers are curtailed by seventy-five percent. You should maintain the discretion over what will be taken away for the evening. If all of the marks were in the Needs Work category, all of his reinforcers should disappear for the afternoon and evening. The good news is that he gets to start all over tomorrow. This is what provides incentive to do better. Sooner or later he will get tired of living without reinforcers and will increase his attempts to earn them on a daily basis. You should be certain to expect that he will have numerous excuses for why all of the ratings were bad at first. Emphasize that you are willing to go only by the teacher's marks. All other excuses will be viewed simply as that—excuses.

If you have an elementary school child, you might want to ask the teachers three or four questions for the morning hours and repeat the questions for the afternoon hours. This will give you some idea of whether or not your child is experiencing difficulty all day or just in the morning or afternoon. This may allow you to help the teachers tailor a more specific strategy for her. You'll find a sample done for morning and afternoon on the next page.

DAILY FEEDBACK SHEET FOR (YOUR CHILD'S NAME)

Day of Week: M T W TH F   DATE:

Morning

	GREAT JOB	OKAY	NEEDS WORK
Did not disrupt others	____	____	____
Acted in a cooperative manner	____	____	____
Handed in any assignments due	____	____	____
Appeared to pay attention	____	____	____

Afternoon

	GREAT JOB	OKAY	NEEDS WORK
Did not disrupt others	____	____	____
Acted in a cooperative manner	____	____	____
Handed in any assignments due	____	____	____
Appeared to pay attention	____	____	____

Signature_____

Again, note that the sheet can be filled out rapidly. Be careful to check the signature and marks to see if your child has been filling them out. It is best to let him know that you intend to call his teacher about the sheets or meet with the teacher on occasion to go over the results. The cagey parent will also keep several copies of the sheets in a safe place, because highly oppositional children have been known to search out and destroy the originals so that their parents don't have copies to give to them to take to school.

The sheet for middle school and high school is necessarily a bit more complex, because it requires that the student be rated by up to seven teachers each day. An example follows.

DAILY FEEDBACK SHEET FOR (YOUR CHILD'S NAME)

Please use the following scale: 1 = Good Job 2 = Okay   3 = Needs Work

DAY OF WEEK: M T W TH F   DATE:

	Class Period						
	1	2	3	4	5	6	7
Did not disrupt others	—	—	—	—	—	—	—
Acted in a cooperative manner	—	—	—	—	—	—	—
Handed in any assignments due	—	—	—	—	—	—	—
Appeared to pay attention	—	—	—	—	—	—	—

You can see that the form is simple to fill out. If your child comes home on a daily basis with mostly ratings of one or two, you should congratulate him. However, if more than four of the slots show ratings of three, you may wish to curtail his reinforcers. Obviously, the more ratings of three your child receives, the more you will be forced to withhold once he gets home from school.

This is certain to increase the amount of work you have to cram into your day. But, using feedback sheets gives you a continuous source of information that you would not have otherwise. You should go over the sheets nightly with your child and make sure that he understands why you have had to remove some of his reinforcers. As we've said, expect excuses and be ready to pay little attention to them. Feel free to make your own copy of these sheets, and modify it in any way that might help.

The Struggle over "No"

There are always going to be times when you have to exercise absolute limits over oppositional children, times when no compromise is possible because what she is asking or demanding is just too absurd. "No" is the worst word in the English language for oppositionals, unless it is coming from their own lips. They tend to take it personally and see it as proof that you are purposefully setting out to frustrate them or make them mad. Learning to accept it with equanimity is essential.

Oppositional children and teenagers are rarely aware of the direction their attitude and behavior take when told "no." Like most of us, once they become angry they switch over to automatic pilot, and off they go. They may accuse you of being a bad parent or tell you that they will do what they want regardless of what you say. As my then three-year-old told my wife one day, "You're a bad, bad momma."

Since hearing the word "no" is the thing that will make defiant children act the most oppositionally, you must think about how you yourself intend to act when setting absolute limits. Remember, the cardinal rule of being around oppositional children and teenagers is not taking their oppositional assault on your authority personally. Keep in mind that all of their defenses have evolved to prevent you from preventing them from doing what they want to do.

Although they might fly at us with considerable fury, if we lose control in return it sends the message that no one is in control. This is an especially bad message for young children to get. When structure dissolves in front of their eyes, as it must seem to when you explode, yell, and act out of control, their own internal level of anxiety increases. As their anxiety increases, so does their defensiveness. They must protect themselves from the frightening idea that you are out of control and therefore unable to protect them. When their defenses increase, they get more oppositional, since it is their main defense mechanism. That's why it does absolutely no good to yell at oppositional children when you are in the throes of a fight. It only makes them more defensive, which makes them more oppositional, which makes you yell even louder, and round and round it goes and where it stops, sadly, nobody knows.

It is a bit different with teenagers. By the time they are eleven or so, they no longer seem to have strong, conscious fears of abandonment. They have begun to live within the fantasy that they can take care of themselves, so yelling and screaming and acting out of control yourself doesn't seem to make them feel quite as unsafe as it did when they were younger. Rather, it just makes them resent you more, because in their minds really strong adults don't lose control. In their minds, really strong adults have the heroic stoicism of a Clint Eastwood character. Although he might get angry, he never gets out of control.

When you say "no" and a fight ensues, it is important to see your teenager's insults as an attempt to throw you off track so that he can exploit your anger, hurt, or confusion. If he can get you mad enough, then he can justify storming out of the house and go do whatever it was that you told him he couldn't go do. Better still, if he can upset you enough so that you go storming out of the house, then he has definitely won.

There is some advice that I give to certain children that comes into play in these situations. When I meet a child who is being tormented by bullies, I ask him if he would be willing to believe anything I said if he knew in advance that I was a bad guy who was going to try to hurt his feelings and make him feel bad about himself. Chances are he will tell me that he would not be willing to listen to me, knowing this. I then explain that this is the way he must learn to think about bullies. The bully's sole intent is to embarrass others and make them feel bad about themselves. I'll tell him that bullies are like skunks. They may look kind of furry and friendly at times, but sooner or later they're going to spray you.

When we apply this logic to the insults of oppositional teenagers, we can see that we must not take them seriously because their sole intent is to prevent us from exercising parental power and influence. Rather than getting caught up arguing about the names they call us or the negative descriptions they offer us of ourselves, it is better to stand back and say, "I'm sorry, the answer is still no."

REINFORCING COMPETENT BEHAVIOR

Let's assume for a moment that you have been working with your child, using all of the techniques we've discussed so far. And let's assume that your work has been successful—your child is coming back under your control. Now you have to face the question of how to keep the progress going. The best tools for this are what psychologists refer to as "shaping procedures."

Assume for a moment that you wish to have me make more

frequent eye contact when I talk to you. You might try just telling me to do this, but if I'm oppositional I'll argue with you about it. Instead, you might try praising me whenever you find me making eye contact. The idea behind this is that if you deliver a type of praise I value close on the heels of my making eye contact, you increase the chance that I will do the behavior again. The next few sections offer some guidelines for reinforcing competent behavior.

Catch Them Being Good

The various punishment techniques we've discussed so far are meant to help the parent get the attention of the oppositional children or teenagers and to decrease the frequency of their negative behaviors. I hope you hear this next sentence clearly and emphatically: You won't be able to help your child or teenager create positive new behaviors through punishment alone. Instead you also need to praise positive conduct. If you catch them being good and praise them while they are being good, you set the stage for them to continue in a positive direction. This means that you have to make decisions in advance about what types of behaviors you hope to see and that you have to have a clear idea of what type of reinforcement your child or teenager values.

Let me give you an idea of how clear targets for behavior and well-defined reinforcers can combine to create behavior change. I recently began to work with a thoroughly oppositional twelve-year-old male with truly poor social skills. He answered almost all questions with "I don't know" or with a shrug of the shoulders. The behaviors that I wished to see him do more frequently were making eye contact and attempting to formulate answers to my questions. I also needed to come up with a reinforcer that he would value. Like most boys his age, he placed a high priority on money. I told him that when I was pleased with his behavior I would flip a coin to him, and that he could keep it. I told him that it might be a nickel, dime, or quarter and that I wouldn't tell him how often I would flip the coin to him.

When I caught him making eye contact, I flipped a coin to him. This immediately reinforced the notion in his mind that eye contact equaled money, and his eye contact with me improved immediately. We talked for a few minutes, and he began to try to answer my questions, not to just shrug "I don't know," so I began to flip more money his way. By the end of the session he had made somewhere between two and three dollars, was making eye contact, and was talking.

His mother's response was two-fold. She was surprised and elated that he interacted with me so well. But she was fearful that she would have to bribe him to get him to talk. Her concern was reasonable. I told her that the coin flip was just a game that I play with kids like him for a brief period to help them get up and running with improved social skills. Once I can see that their social skills are developing and they are trying to hold conversations, I begin to replace the coins with verbal praise. This is precisely how it worked with this particular young man. I had to use the coin flip with him for probably three sessions total. It cost me around six or seven dollars in change. It costs me nothing today when I congratulate him on making good eye contact and trying to give clear answers to my questions.

His skills have continued to develop. On occasion, he tries to answer me with "I don't know," but I remind him that I've seen him use his verbal skills too many times now to believe he can't respond to my questions. His mother also uses this line of logic when he tries to use "I don't know" at home. She tells him, "I've seen you talk to Dr. Riley. You have to talk to me too."

I offer this case to illustrate the power of catching the child or teenager doing the behavior that you desire and delivering an immediate reward. In most cases you will not have to deliver a reward nearly so tangible as money. You will find that some children respond quickly to verbal praise, such as "I really like it when you look at me when you talk. The way you just did that was great!" With older children and teenagers you have to be more subtle. "I like it when you act friendly. It makes me want to try harder too."

Round of Applause

A variation of catching children under ten being good is to announce to them that you really like what they just did and hope they will continue to do it. Then tell them that because they are being so good, they have earned a round of applause. At this point you clap. You can also use this in a delayed fashion, such as telling them you have learned of something they did earlier that was good and offer applause as a reward.

I am aware that on the surface this may seem like a pretty goofy idea. We fail to remember, however, that receiving an ovation is a pretty common fantasy. Children like it a lot, particularly the younger ones. When my own children were younger and did something that my wife or I especially valued, such as helping a peer who was sad or who had been hurt or bullied, or when they mastered a difficult school task, we would have them stand up at the dinner table and announce to the family what they had done. Then we would all deliver a round of applause. Their little faces would invariably break out in smiles, and they would rightfully feel the pride of their accomplishments. A secondary offshoot of this technique is that it will leave both the parent and the child with some particularly sweet memories.

Physical Reinforcers

Most children who have yet to reach puberty have a strong desire for physical contact with adults. Children who have been well loved will spontaneously climb into your lap, lean against you, or take your hand. They have a special affinity for receiving hugs, getting high fives, having their hair tousled by you, being patted on the back, and so on. You should feel free to use these as rewards with your own children. They are excellent reinforcers because they are dramatic, free, and can be delivered on the spot. My only caution is that you be sensitive to the context in which you deliver the reinforcer. Your eleven-year-old on the edge of puberty, may love it if you hug him when you're alone but may treat you like you're radioactive when he's around his friends. Mothers may find that as their sons approach puberty, they will accept physical reinforcement from their fathers, or other significant males, but no longer from them. Fathers may see this same pattern with their daughters. Although heartbreaking to parents, this is entirely normal. The ground rule is to continue to use physical reinforcers as long as your children give you signals that they value them. Be sensitive to their signals because they will try to let you know nonverbally that they are too old for hugs and high fives before they will come right out and say it.

Visible Reinforcers

Another technique to use with young children, those below age eight, is to cut a star out of construction paper or light cardboard. Tell your child that when she is doing a great job—being competent—you will keep the star up on the wall in a prominent place, such as the kitchen. Sit down with her and decorate the star. Let her color it, put glitter on it, and personalize it in any way she wishes. If her behavior turns negative in a marked manner, let her know that you will have to take the star down and that it cannot be put back up until you are happy with her behavior again. Set a standard of where you expect several hours of normal, acceptable behavior before you return the star to the wall. Don't fall into the trap of putting it back up five minutes after you took it down because you don't want to hurt her feelings. The purpose of the star is to indicate in a visible way that she is making good decisions and managing her own behavior at the top of her ability. Think of it like any other award. If everyone at your company was given a certificate of award tomorrow, it would have little value. When only a few people get it because of high performance, it has value far beyond its physical worth.

Increased Access to Major Reinforcers

Your teenager is not likely to respond to hanging stars on the wall and giving her high fives. With teenagers, as with children, you use what they value to shape new behavior. Just as you may have to totally remove your seventeen-year-old's access to the car in order to get her attention, so too can you increase her roaming and curfew limits for displaying competent behavior. The simple but important point here is to make sure she realizes that you are letting her stay out later because of the competency of her decisions and behavior.

You can use this technique with most children and with a wide variety of objects. "I'm going to let you use my stereo because the way you've been acting lately tells me you can handle it." "We're going to let you ride your bike over to the next neighborhood because we trust you to make good decisions." "You can go ahead and surf the Internet without me here. I trust you to stay away from the bad stuff." And so on.

Several cautions are in order. Most children and all teenagers will press you to consistently increase their access to major reinforcers out of the belief that simply getting older equates to increased access. Part of their competency training is to tell them that access is earned and does not come on demand. Avoid the following three major mistakes that are possible when considering competency. The first is giving your child or teenager undeserved increases in access to major goodies. The second is failing to increase their access when they are acting in a highly competent manner. The third is not rescinding a privilege when a child or teenager's behavior no longer warrants having access.

TEENAGERS AND PART-TIME WORK

I've included this section because it is a pet peeve, an issue I see creating trouble in many families. It goes like this: If your oppositional teenager is working and earning his own money and manages to stay employed long enough to save some of it, chances are he will think that because the money is his, you cannot tell him when he can leave the house to go spend it. This is a good example of bad teenager logic.

A variation on this theme is the attitude that because he has a job, he may now leave the house whenever he wishes. You should not be surprised if he tells you that he has to leave the house to be at work, when this is not the case.

Part-time work for teenagers is a privilege that must be earned by displaying competent behavior. If your teenager is not achieving academically at a level commensurate with her ability, if she has a bad attitude at home, or if she has failed to heed your rules on a consistent basis, then she has not earned the right to take a part-time job. If she is allowed to take a part-time job and then begins to spend her money foolishly, or on drugs and alcohol, she may be forced to forfeit the job. She will tell you that you cannot make her quit. You may then remind her that her employer will no longer make her welcome if you call and say that she does not have your permission to work.

As with all of the rules and ideas we have discussed thus far, there are probably hundreds of other points to consider about training your child to act in a competent manner, a manner that will leave you willing to increase their freedom, responsibility, and funds. You should feel free to add your ideas to those above and use them with your children. The final point about competency training, however, is to make sure that you, the parent, see clearly that training a child to act in a competent manner is much like training him to hit a baseball. You must be actively involved with him, and you have to practice, practice, practice. You cannot tell an oppositional child simply to change. You have to present him with clear demands for change, clear restrictions for refusal to modify negative behaviors, and clear rewards for acting in a competent manner.

CHAPTER SEVEN

Oppositional Defiant Disorder and Other Conditions

To make things even more complicated, let me remind you that oppositional defiant disorder can coexist with other disorders. In most cases it is perfectly appropriate to continue to treat oppositional behavior that coexists with another disorder with the methods discussed thus far. In some cases, however, there are special considerations you'll want to be aware of.

ATTENTION DEFICIT HYPERACTIVITY DISORDER

The bookstore shelves these days are bulging with books on attention deficit hyperactivity disorder, which is also commonly referred to as attention deficit disorder. You may also have heard the abbreviations ADHD or ADD. Although there are technical distinctions to be made, essentially these terms refer to a neurological condition that inhibits one's ability to remain focused and on task. The disorder comes in several flavors. Some ADHD children are quiet and keep to themselves at the back of the classroom. Although they might nod at the teacher and smile pleasantly, they aren't hearing a word. Others with it are like tiny tornadoes tearing about the room in unfocused, chaotic activity. You can't help but notice them in the classroom because of the inordinate time they take up with discipline-related issues. A surprising number of children in gifted and talented programs have ADHD. It seems to be more prominent in boys than in girls, although some investigators suspect that girls, because of their faster social development and superior social skills, develop coping mechanisms that help them deal with their impulsive urges better than their male counterparts.

The underbelly of ADHD is that a large percentage of these children and teenagers have a marked oppositional behavior pattern to go along with their attention issues. Unfortunately both issues become more difficult to treat because of the interference of the other. For example, it is hard to have a conversation with an oppositional eight-year-old about the impact of her defiance on the family peace when she can't sit still for more than five seconds at a time. She's likely to be looking around constantly while you are talking and to have her feet tapping and her hands fiddling with each other while she should be making eye contact.

It is likewise difficult to talk to this same child about improving her ability to complete tasks when she is prone to inform you that you can't tell her what to do and if you try to she won't listen, so there!

When children have multiple problems, it is important to treat all their symptoms. The traditional treatments for attention issues have little impact upon oppositional attitude, and the treatments recommended in this book for oppositional attitude will have little impact on attention deficits. Given that oppositional behavior is often seen in the ADHD children and teens, many physicians who prescribe medications for their ADHD symptoms do so also hoping that their oppositional behavior will decrease as well. On occasion, medication may help both sets of symptoms, but more frequently not, in my experience as a child psychologist.

Fortunately, most physicians who prescribe treatment for their ADHD/oppositional-defiant disorder patients have become aware that successfully treating ADHD requires a multiprofessional approach. Few operate with the idea that stimulants and other medications are magic bullets. The most successful treatment models involve communication between the parents, teachers, pediatricians, child psychiatrists, and child psychologists or other therapist. All of these individuals make suggestions to parents and to each other regarding not only ADHD but the oppositional behavior as well. Of this group, however, the ones with the most experience and training in helping the parents deal with oppositional behavior when it coexists with ADHD will be those trained primarily in behavioral health issues, such as psychologists, clinical social workers, and licensed professional counselors. When I consult with parents of children with both ADHD and oppositional defiant disorder, they get the ADHD treatment established first. The insight a child needs to overcome oppositional behavior and thinking patterns is not likely to happen until the child is better able to focus on and think about their behavior and the responses it creates others. Once the ADHD treatment seems to be working, it is reasonable to begin using the methods outlined in this book for treating oppositional behavior.

MOOD DISORDERS

Oppositional behavior and mood disorders such as depression or anxiety often go hand in hand. One does not create the other. Although it is true to say that they coexist, it is important to recognize that they also interact. If you take the moodiness, hopelessness, and anger that can be part of childhood depression and combine them with all of the thinking and behavior patterns of the opposi-tional child, you can see that the combination can be particularly painful to all involved. The result is a child who is not only angry and oppositional, but who is angry and oppositional in a depressive, hopeless manner.

Depression

Sometimes a child can be so oppositional that you overlook the possibility that she is depressed. The problem is that, although you might be doing all the right things to treat her oppositionality, you will be doomed to fail because her depression will keep her in a rut. Because of this risk, you need to know what signs to look for.

The most obvious signs are statements or threats about wanting to die. There are other, more subtle signs, however. Children and teens express depression in a different manner from adults. They can become agitated and angry and act out through yelling and scream-ing, calling names, and starting fights. This makes them look opposi-tional instead of depressed. Additionally, they experience disturbances in their sleep pattern like oversleeping, waking up fre-quently, or chronic nightmares. They might display changes in their eating patterns. They might eat more than normal or less than nor-mal. They may become apathetic, no longer seeming to care about grades, friends, dating, or sports. They may lose the ability to enjoy the things they used to enjoy. They may seem listless, bored, and tired all of the time. It is not uncommon for depressed children and teenagers to have vague physical complaints, such as unexplained stomachaches, headaches, and back pains.

The treatment of choice for childhood depression is counseling. Medications should be used only when it seems that the depression is of the resistant type or may be of biological origin. In general, most depressed children and teenagers respond to any type of psychotherapy that allows them to examine the negative beliefs that they harbor about themselves. Although it is true that they might have a great deal of anger directed toward a parent or other significant person, in my experience most depressed children and teens I have met are mired in a process of not liking themselves and using any mistake they might make as proof that they are worthless. Once they are able to see the fallacy of this type of thinking, they move out of depression.

If you believe that your child or adolescent suffers from both oppositional behavior and depression, it is important to treat the depression first. Think of depression as a boat anchor attached to the soul of your child—she will not be able to move forward with developing new, less oppositional viewpoints and behaviors as long as she is weighed down by the hopelessness and negative self-image that are part of depression. Only after her mood is improved can you expect a change in her oppositional behavior.

Anxiety

Anxiety, another type of mood disorder, is equally troubling in the oppositional child or teenager. Anxiety is more difficult to treat than depression because it is often not as consciously perceived as depression. Most depressed children and teens can tell you at least something about why they feel depressed, but anxious children and teens typically can't tell you why they feel anxious.

Anxiety and oppositional behavior interact in a particularly difficult way. Oppositional children are often vigilant, spending much of their spare time scanning their environments for indications of danger or insult. When anxiety is added to the mixture, the result is an oppositional child who can seem paranoid, often insisting that you are purposefully out to make him unhappy or to frustrate him.

What you should realize is that anxiety is often a safety-related disorder. Working underneath the surface of anxious individuals is the fear that something horrible and beyond their control is about to transpire. What they dread is too horrible to think about consciously, so they exclude it from their mind. I know one highly anxious and oppositional ten-year-old, for example, who has become phobic about going to school. When he is at school he screams, moans, and groans so loud about the pain in his stomach that he has to be sent home. He does not have the stomach pains at home, and consequently everyone has come to believe that he is faking in order to skip school. To try to get at what was bothering him I gave him a battery of psychological tests, one in which he had to look at pictures of people engaged in various activities. His task was to look at a picture and then tell me a story about it. The theory is that, since the pictures have no right or wrong answers, kids will project on them what they are unconsciously thinking. His stories were full of death themes, kids getting stabbed or killed, kids getting shot in the back while riding home on their bikes, kids getting diseases and simply dying. With fears such as these lurking in his mind, there should be little surprise that he feels safe only at home.

Anxious oppositional children dig their heels in and refuse to try anything new because it takes them out of the safety of their already-established patterns and habits. They spend all their time trying to make themselves feel safe, or worrying about something bad that might happen. They borrow trouble, so to speak, because they worry about things that haven't happened yet. They begin to constrict their worlds, living in less and less space. The fewer places they have to go, the safer they feel. As they descend into anxiety, they might go from freely roaming their neighborhood to being afraid to leave their rooms.

The causes for such childhood anxiety are numerous, and I am increasingly disturbed by the stories that children tell me today about gangs in the hallways of their middle schools, about high-schoolers packing knives and guns in their backpacks, and about drive-by shootings. These things rattle our children to the core.

The cure? Again, I favor behavioral methods over medicine, although such a subject would be a book all in itself. In general, anxious children must gradually be reintroduced into the environments or activities that frighten them. They know it is important to keep trying, but it is too much like being told to pet the big dog after having been bitten, or being told to go back on the roller coaster after having the wits scared out of you. You are not likely to get your oppositional, anxious child to try new behaviors or to come to understand the impact of his oppositional behavior upon others as long as he is concerned with his safety. The first move, as I noted above with depression, is to have his anxiety disorder treated, with the hope that you can move on afterward to changing his oppositional behavior.

LEARNING DISABILITIES

A significant number of the children I evaluate for learning problems also display oppositional behavior. Children and teenagers with learning disabilities should not be confused with children who are not smart. Children with learning disabilities are often quite bright in ways that schools do not value or place emphasis on. They are aware that their peers pick up certain types of information better than they and, because of this, develop oppositional attitudes in order to compensate for what they are unable to do in the classroom.

As in the ADHD example, treatment and remediation for learning disabilities will have little or no effect on oppositional attitude, and the two should be treated as separate issues. As with any child with a learning disability, however, the specific nature of the disability must be taken into account when trying to plan treatment for oppositional behavior. You would be foolish, for instance, to ask your son who has great difficulty reading to read this book. It would be much better to engage him in a role play about how oppositional individuals act toward others around them. If you own or can borrow a video camera, it might prove terrifically interesting to have him make a film about a day in the life of an oppositional teenager, how he views others, how others view him, and so on. Likewise, he may also gain more insight into his oppositional behavior through artwork, such as drawing portraits of oppositional and nonoppositional people and analyzing the differences.

Your task with the learning disabled child is to find the learning modalities that they are the strongest in and exploit those strengths. Remember that children with learning disabilities should never be punished or criticized for their difficulties with academic tasks. I have yet to meet a child who didn't really want to learn.

BEHAVIOR DISORDERS

Most school systems have programs for children who cannot flourish in the regular classroom because of factors that have little to do with intellect. The term "Emotionally Disabled" is used by professionals in the field of special education to encompass any of a number of mental health diagnostic categories. Children with the "ED" label might include the oppositional, defiant children we have been describing thus far. Children who are too disruptive to their peers, perhaps due to attention deficit hyperactivity disorder, sometimes receive the "ED" label at school and are placed into smaller, more intensive classrooms in order to control their behavior and to enhance their ability to learn. Children who are highly aggressive, highly anxious, or who are withdrawn can also be labeled "ED" and placed into learning environments where they are more likely to progress than in the mainstream classroom.

The real advantage of being identified for special educational services is that the child will receive intensive, personalized attention from the school system. The flaw in the system, certainly not the fault of the schools, is that no budget is large enough to create special programs for each mental health diagnostic category. Because of this, everyone tends to get lumped under the "ED" label.

The most difficult aspect of providing adequate treatment for these children is to make sure that all of their emotional problems have been diagnosed and treated with acceptable methods, something that is far beyond the capability of any school system. Parents often unfairly expect schools to function as mental health systems, which is impossible. Treatment for emotional problems should be done by mental health professionals, just as teaching should be done by professionals in the field of education.

CONDUCT DISORDER

Although it may seem that oppositional children and teenagers are nearly impossible to deal with, they need to be placed into proper perspective by comparing them to children and teenagers with conduct disorder, a polite term in the field of psychopathology for "young sociopath."

Be careful not to confuse children with oppositional defiant disorder with children with conduct disorder. They may look alike at first, but you must realize that children with conduct disorder will do everything oppositional children do, and then some. If oppositional children can be called amateurs, conduct disorder children are professionals. Most oppositional children don't grow up and go to jail. Conduct disorder children have an express ticket there, with early stops at juvenile court, youth centers, and detention facilities. Oppositional children might tease your dog or cat, but conduct disorder children will torture it. Opposition children might develop early interests in sex. Conduct disorder teenagers commit rape. Oppositional teenagers might like to hang out on the edge of gangs in order to make themselves look tough. Conduct disorder teenagers will kill someone because he or she is wearing the wrong color bandanna.

Years ago I interviewed one of the small number of children I have talked to who have committed murders prior to age fourteen. In this case the murderer was thirteen; he had shot another young man in order to steal his portable stereo. I recall asking him why he had killed the other young man, hoping to learn more about what went on in his mind. I remember him looking at me with eyes devoid of emotion, sorrow, or guilt. His answer was concise and to the point: "So I could take the box." It was that simple. He saw something the other child had and decided upon the fastest way to get it. Chilling.

Children and adolescents with conduct disorder leave you with the impression of having no feelings about the bad things they have done. They appear absent of guilt and seem to operate without conscience. They do this because they do not see fellow human beings when they look at others. They see only objects, there to be used in whatever way necessary to gratify their needs. They can harm someone viciously and five minutes later be having fun with their friends. I mention them so you will not make the mistake of thinking that your ordinary oppositional child will grow up to be a criminal or a killer. When placed into perspective with the conduct disorder child or adolescent, the oppositional child does not look nearly so bad.

Treatment of these children is outside the scope of this book. I should indicate, however, that in reality they receive little treatment because they are on a rapid downward slope from very early in their lives. Given that they cannot confine their behavior to societal standards, they are kicked out of the regular classroom early in their academic careers. They typically are placed in the Emotionally

Disabled setting where, paradoxically, they have contact only with others who share their jaded and aggressive viewpoint. As a group they tend to end up in jail at young ages, where they are often abused and further hardened. They are repeat offenders of violent crimes, with high levels of drug and alcohol abuse, as well as spouse and child abuse. When you talk to them they always have an excuse for what they have done or will claim to have done nothing at all, even in the face of overwhelming evidence to the contrary. Or, they will try to convince you that the person they harmed either brought it on themselves, or deserved it.

If you recognize your child in this description, immediately get him into long-term contact with a strong same-sex therapist, role model, or mentor and make sure every strong adult you know spends time with him so that he learns to trust and enjoy adults rather than see them as enemies. Insist that he learn to develop friendships with prosocial kids and do not accept his attempts to become part of a peer group with antisocial leanings. Do your best not to lose him to the streets, as young sociopaths attract each other like magnets. Once they are in gangs, they become lost to you so rapidly it is breathtaking. Expose him early in life to the great religious traditions so that he develops a conscience. Take him to libraries and museums and art galleries so that hanging out on the street does not become his major form of fun. Do not allow him to listen only to the destructive and profoundly violent music that is currently popular and that will entice him into believing that violence is manly. Talk to him openly about the messages contained in the music he listens to, the messages that glorify guns, violence, and abuse of women. Expose him to other musical forms so that he can realize he does not have to look to violence-worshiping musicians as his role models. Ask him why rich rap musicians move to cloistered suburbs if urban violence and hard attitudes are so great. Ask him why cokehead grungers kill themselves if there is so much truth to be found in staying stoned. And finally, follow the suggestions in this book on competency training. If he is not outfitted early on with the attitude that the good things in life are earned through competency and effort, he has little chance of surviving his own personality characteristics.

CHAPTER EIGHT

The Long–Term Outlook for the Defiant Child

CHILDREN WITH oppositional defiant disorder have not been formally studied long enough to say with any assurance what the outlook for them is. However, many psychologists and other mental health professionals will probably agree with the notion that their futures depend on the level of their oppositionality. As we have noted, oppositional children should not be mistaken for young sociopaths, whose prospects are negative by any standards. Children who are moderately oppositional, the types who drive you up the wall at home with their constant arguing, bickering, and pressing of limits but who have managed to have basically good relationships with their peers, are likable enough to get invited to do things by others their age, and are not getting booted out of school due to behavior problems probably have the same general chances for success as any other child.

I refer to these children as the ones with a "movable ceiling" of behavior. At home they may leave you exasperated beyond belief, but they have the insight and ability to elevate their behavior and act in totally appropriate ways when outside the home. My impression from having followed a number of these children over a period of years is that they mature and do well. I often joke to their parents that if they make it to age twenty-five, everything will be okay. My real message to the parents is for them to take heart in the knowledge that their son or daughter acts much better everywhere else. This shows intact insight and good decision-making abilities that, though not being used at home, are still there.

Up the scale a notch on the next level of oppositionality, we might see a child who is still doing relatively well in the outside world, but who is violent, verbally abusive, or prone to simply come and go as he pleases at home. This is the level where real trouble starts. If such children learn from their home experience that they can use violence, verbal abuse, or open defiance as a way to get what they want, it is more likely that their chances for outside success will fade. At some point they will begin to seek out peers who are acting the same way. Association with such a peer group has a way of reinforcing their home behavior. Soon they get brave enough to begin telling off their teachers, then others. In such cases, it is important to stem the tide of their oppositional behavior so that it does not spill out of the family setting.

Some children are openly oppositional and defiant from a very early age and cannot hide or modify their behavior when away from their home settings. I see any number of teenagers who, even though they have never met me before, are surly and negative toward me. I ask them directly why they are being so impolite, given that I have done nothing to them. Their first answers usually go something like "I don't want to go see no shrink." I let them know that if I was their age, I probably wouldn't want to go see a shrink either, but that it wouldn't be cause for me to act in a highly unfriendly way toward a complete stranger. The ones who can lighten up and interact in a more appropriate manner usually have the better chance of succeeding in the outside world. The ones who remain angry, negative, and oppositional are the ones who almost invariably act this way everywhere they go. They are oppositional twenty-four hours a day, seven days a week.

These are the ones who mystify the adults around them. Frequently they seem capable enough underneath their oppositional exterior to be successful. However, they will not give up the oppositional attitude long enough to allow success to happen. Individuals like this often remain on the margins. They alienate everyone around them by being negative and argumentative, and they fail to see the necessity of modifying their behavior. I have known individuals in my personal life who displayed this behavior pattern as teenagers. Although they may have managed to modify it slightly, they remained negative and argumentative at mid-life.

The notch above this is the pattern of continuous oppositionality combined with a propensity to act in a violent manner when angry or frustrated. Here the line between the oppositional personality type and the sociopathic personality type becomes pretty thin. The only remaining question is whether they begin to represent a general, ongoing danger to others. It is bad enough that highly oppositional types may represent a danger to their family members when they are angered, but at least they do not typically go looking for reasons to harm others. Sociopaths actively seek others to harm.

THERAPY AND THE OPPOSITIONAL CHILD OR TEENAGER

You may find that you are able to handle the moderately oppositional child on your own, without consulting mental health professionals. As we've said, the long-term outlook for these children and teenagers can be quite positive. If you find, however, that your child or teen's behavior is so oppositional that it thoroughly disrupts family functioning, you should seek professional help.

A huge percentage of the children and teenagers who see professional mental health counselors are there because of their oppositional behavior. There are two patterns I see when parents bring these kids to my office. The first pattern is the instant turnaround. This used to mystify me, but I think I have come to understand it.

Years ago I had an elementary school teacher call me to discuss a young man from her class. She said to me, "I don't know what you're doing, but it's working miracles. Keep it up." I mumbled my appreciation for her feedback and assured her I would continue what I was doing. The truth is that I had seen him only once and had no idea what I might have done to cause such rapid change.

I had an almost identical phone call about a year later. This caused me to have to think further about what was going on. As nice as it would have been to think that I was working some sort of magic with these children, I had to remain doubtful of any such explanation. Slowly I began to understand that the sheer act of a parent taking a child to therapy sends a profound message to the child. It says clearly, "We are now in control. Things must change." The fact that the child got this message had nothing to do with me and everything to do with the parents. This gets back to the earlier parts of this book where we talked about structure. Closing structure in around a child almost always decreases his symptoms.

Instant change can often fool parents into pulling a child out of therapy too quickly. If you seek counseling and you see an immediate change, do not be lulled into thinking that two or three sessions have somehow "cured" a lifelong behavior problem. The people who run the managed health care industry would love to have you believe such a claim, but unfortunately you would likely learn the hard way that quick fixes do not last. Do yourself a favor: Keep your child in therapy until you see a good, solid three months of behavior that, although not perfect, is more within the normal range of behavior for children your child's age. Keep in mind that he might be in therapy for three months before you see reemergence of normal behavior. Once you see three months of solid progress, it may be reasonable to decrease the frequency of your meetings. If you decrease to twice per month and the negative behavior comes back, you have decreased too soon. Once you are on a decreased schedule, usually one session every two to three weeks, stay on it until you can reasonably say there is little difference between your child's behavior and that of his peers.

You may find that your child goes back to his oppositional ways during his major developmental shifts, and if this is the case, therapy can always be reinstituted for as long as necessary. You might, for example, have your six-year-old reined in only to find that around age nine, when he becomes considerably more independent, back comes oppositionality. It might go away again with effort, only to emerge once puberty begins, around age eleven. You might go through the battle again, and things will return to peacefulness until age thirteen or fourteen. After that, oppositional patterns can come back around age seventeen. These can be remarkably intense, heralding the teenager's need to be out on his own. You should expect a decrease in oppositional behavior as the teen years end and the twenties begin. Once oppositional types are out in the "real world," many are often forced to moderate their behavior, finding that most college professors or bosses won't tolerate it. Neither will most of the people they want to date.

The second pattern to watch for is an attempt by the child or teenager to disrupt therapy right off the bat. Don't be fooled by this. Any therapist who is trained to work with children and teenagers knows that the start can sometimes be rocky, and you have to allow time for the client-therapist relationship to develop. I have had teenagers come into my office on many occasions, flop down with their arms crossed in defiance, and give me a look that says, "You can't make me talk." Sometimes they even say this. I reply that they are probably right; I can't make them talk. I let them know that I've never been able to make anybody talk and that I don't believe any therapist who says that he or she can make someone talk. Then I ask without criticism or pressure what sort of things they like to do, what kind of music they like, and so on. Therapy with a child or adolescent emerges out of a relationship, and relationships take time to form. Given that oppositional children and teenagers can be a wary lot, do not expect therapy with them to go quickly.

FINDING THE RIGHT THERAPIST

School counselors and pediatricians are probably the best sources for recommending therapists skilled in work with children and adolescents. You should also consider asking your friends if they know any good therapists from direct experience. Pay no attention to yellow page ads, because advertisement size tells you only about a therapist's or group's advertising budget. Be careful when calling a referral service. Therapists listed with such services often pay a fee to the service. You should ask if this is the case. Keep in mind that the operator giving you names doesn't know them from Adam or Eve and most assuredly knows nothing of their work. Remain cautious of names given you by insurance companies. The list of providers in an insurance company's handbook is just a list of therapists who have agreed to accept the insurance company's discounted hourly pay rate in return for being a provider for the company. The idea is that the insurance carrier can guarantee the therapist that she will be allowed to see their clients if the therapist lowers her fee. At the same time, be aware that about every therapist out there, myself included, has been forced to make these agreements in order to stay in business. The insurance companies have us all over a particular barrel: Accept a discounted fee rate or forget about seeing our insured. And, to their credit, not all insurance carriers attempt to interfere with treatment or place ridiculous limits on it. Like most therapists, I have a list of insurance companies that I simply will not do business with because of their attempts to intrude into the therapy process or their attempts to make coverage so brief that no work of any depth is possible.

The best advice I can give you is to go interview the therapist you are considering seeing. Many therapists will be happy to sit with you for a half hour, at no fee, and answer your questions about their training, approach, expertise in the particular problems your child or teenager is displaying, and so on. I urge anyone who is seeking a therapist for an oppositional child or teenager to ask the therapist what percentage of his case load is made up of children and teenagers. Ask about internships and practicums, which are advanced training stages for therapists. Did he get specific supervision from a senior therapist in working with children? How much of his training case load was composed of children? Did he train in a clinic or hospital that specialized in children? If not, how has he gained his experience with children? One of the things you may be dismayed to learn of the therapy field is that people routinely claim expertise in areas that they are only scantily trained or experienced in. If someone tells you, "Oh yes, I see a small number of children and teenagers," what he is really saying is that he is primarily an adult therapist who fills up the holes in his schedule by seeing kids. As I would not go to my internist to have my tooth fixed, neither would I take my child to someone who is not deeply engaged in work with children.

What sort of therapist should you see? Try to remember that the therapy field is made up of a number of disciplines. Although we may all look the same to the public, we have distinct differences. Psychologists have doctoral degrees (Ph.D., Ed.D., Psy.D., D.Sc.) and are trained in a wide range of therapy techniques. Additionally, they are the only mental health professionals trained to administer and interpret psychological tests. Psychiatrists are physicians who sought specialized training in mental health after completing medical school. They hold M.D. or D.O. degrees. Years ago they did therapy. Today, most don't, or are trained in only one type of therapy. They are the only mental health professionals capable of prescribing medication. Clinical Social Workers typically have master's degrees in social work (MSW), although a small number go on for doctorates. They have historically been the real experts in family therapy, although they are also trained in individual counseling. Licensed Professional Counselors have either master's degrees or doctoral degrees. Like psychologists and social workers, they are trained in a number of therapy techniques for working with individuals and families.

Which of these designations is best for therapists of oppositional children? There is no evidence that therapists trained in any of the mental health disciplines have any edge over therapists from other disciplines when it comes to doing psychotherapy. Like all professions, each has its good and bad apples. The main question should come down to whether or not the particular therapist you see seems to match up well with your child. If she seems to understand the issues at hand and, more importantly, if your child feels understood and seems to value his contact with the therapist, then the chances go up that you have a good match.

Should you ever change therapists? Of course, if it's necessary. If you have had your child in to see someone for at least a month of weekly sessions and your child tells you repeatedly that the therapist is stupid, doesn't understand them, or that they just don't like the therapist, consider changing. No therapist will match with one hundred percent of the clients she meets. If your child doesn't get along with her, it does not mean she is a bad therapist. It simply means that the match between her and your child was not optimal. In the best of cases, the therapist will recognize that the fit is not right and refer you to someone else. This therapeutic match is of the utmost importance because you are playing for high stakes. If your child and his therapist are well matched, you may see amazing changes in behavior and insight. Very little will happen if the match is wrong.

MEDICATIONS

I am not aware of any specific medication that has been devised to curb oppositional behavior. Many children and teenagers take medications for other conditions, however, and these medications may have a beneficial effect in some cases. For example, children and teenagers who are oppositional and who are taking stimulant medication for attention deficit hyperactivity disorder sometimes seem to be less argumentative and touchy. The deeper question here is whether or not their oppositional behavior is part of their attention deficit and not a free standing symptom all its own. You should not expect your physician to prescribe stimulant medications for oppositional behavior. This would be totally unwarranted.

Likewise, oppositional children and teens who also have a diagnosis of depression often seem less on edge and less angry after they begin antidepressants. However, do not expect your physician to prescribe antidepressants for oppositional behavior.

I do not suggest that parents get their hopes up any time soon for a medication used specifically to treat oppositional behavior. It is unlikely that drug companies will put any real effort into developing such medications because oppositional behavior is not thought of as a disease, and many insurance companies do not view it as a real medical disorder. Given this, parents are primarily limited to the behavioral methods we have discussed so far.

FINAL COMMENTS

We should not be discouraged that we cannot wipe out oppositional behavior with a pill. The persistence and strength of will seen in many children and teenagers with ODD are to be admired in a curious way. They are often bright, creative, and inventive. Medications might destroy their positive characteristics along with their negative ones. Out goes the baby with the bath water.

If I may suggest a final intervention, it is to return to the idea of admiring your oppositional child or teen's strength. Be sure to let him know that you like his drive. Although you may not agree with many of the things he does, let him know you find much about him that you would not change even if you could. These positive attributes may be harder to find in some children and adolescents than in others because some can present themselves in a thoroughly negative manner. Be sure to look hard for the good, though. After everything is said and done, it is likely that oppositional children and teenagers fight the world so vigorously because they truly believe that if they don't, the adult world will crush them. Rather than roll over and succumb, they fight out of an attempt to dignify themselves. Although this is admirable, they can only flounder without your guidance, support, and involvement. They do not need you as an enemy.

| INDEX |